Windsor and Habsburg

The British and Austrian
reigning houses
1848–1922

Also by John Van der Kiste

Frederick III: German Emperor 1888 (Alan Sutton 1981)
Queen Victoria's family: a select bibliography (Clover 1982)
Roxeventies: popular music in Britain, 1970–79 (Kawabata 1982)
Dearest Affie. . . : Alfred, Duke of Edinburgh, Queen Victoria's second son, 1844–1900 [with Bee Jordaan] (Alan Sutton 1984)
The Roy Wood story (A & F 1986)
Queen Victoria's children (Alan Sutton 1986)

Windsor and Habsburg

The British and Austrian reigning houses 1848–1922

John Van der Kiste

ALAN SUTTON
1987

Alan Sutton Publishing
Brunswick Road · Gloucester

First published 1987

British Library Cataloguing in Publication Data

Van der Kiste, John
    Windsor and Habsburg : the British and
    Austrian reigning houses, 1848–1922.
    1. Windsor (*House of*)   2. Habsburg (*House of*)
    3.   Great Britain—Foreign relations—
    Austria   4. Austria—Foreign relations
    —Great Britain
    I. Title
    941.081   DA555

    ISBN 0-86299-338-5

Jacket illustration: King Edward VII and Emperor Francis Joseph at the opera, Vienna, 1 September 1903, after a drawing by Edward Cucuel. Private Collection.

Typesetting and origination by
Alan Sutton Publishing Limited.
Photoset Bembo 10/11.
Printed in Great Britain

Contents

Illustrations

Nos. 6a, 9, 12, 14, 15 and 16 are reproduced by kind permission of Mrs R. Prior, Sussex Commemorative Ware Centre, 88 Western Road, Hove, Sussex. The remainder are from private collections.

Acknowledgements

I wish to acknowledge the gracious permission of Her Majesty The Queen to publish certain material of which she owns the copyright.

I am indebted to the following copyright holders for permission to quote from published works: Allen & Unwin Ltd (*Queen Mary*, by James Pope-Hennessy); Collins Harvill (*Uncle of Europe*, and *Victims at Sarajevo*, both by Gordon Brook-Shepherd); Elaine Greene Ltd (*The Eagles Die*, Copyright © 1974 by George R. Marek); Macmillan Ltd (*Letters of the Empress Frederick*, edited by Sir Frederick Ponsonby, and *The Road to Mayerling*, by Richard Barkeley); Unwin Hyman Ltd (*Dearest Child, Dearest Mama, Your dear letter,* and *Darling Child*, all edited by Roger Fulford); and Weidenfeld (Publishers) Ltd (*Imperial adventurer*, by Joan Haslip, and *The last Habsburg,* by Gordon Brook-Shepherd).

Every effort has been made to trace and acknowledge all copyright owners, and apologies are offered to authors and publishers whose rights may have been inadvertently infringed.

My thanks for constant help, advice and encouragement are due to my parents, Wing Commander Guy and Nancy Van der Kiste, and to my niece, Louise Martin; and, for the generous loan of illustrations, to Mrs R. Prior, of the Sussex Commemorative Ware Centre, 88 Western Road, Hove, Sussex.

Foreword

This book is intended as a study of Anglo-Austrian relations as seen through personal and political connections between the families of Queen Victoria and Emperor Francis Joseph. Despite my emphasis on the latter, it is not intended as a chronicle of Habsburg family misfortunes during the long reign of Francis Joseph and the brief rule of his great-nephew and successor Charles. Readers anxious for more detail on episodes such as the inglorious Austrian defeats at Solferino and Königgrätz, the Mayerling tragedy and the assassinations at Sarajevo which precipitated the end of an era in Europe, will find a wealth of relevant titles in the bibliography. Yet a close examination of the period covered, from the year of revolutions to the uncertain post-Great War age, reveals some fascinating sidelights on contemporary royalty which have received little attention from biographers – and until now never in one volume.

The House of Saxe-Coburg Saalfeld, Saxe-Coburg Gotha and Windsor

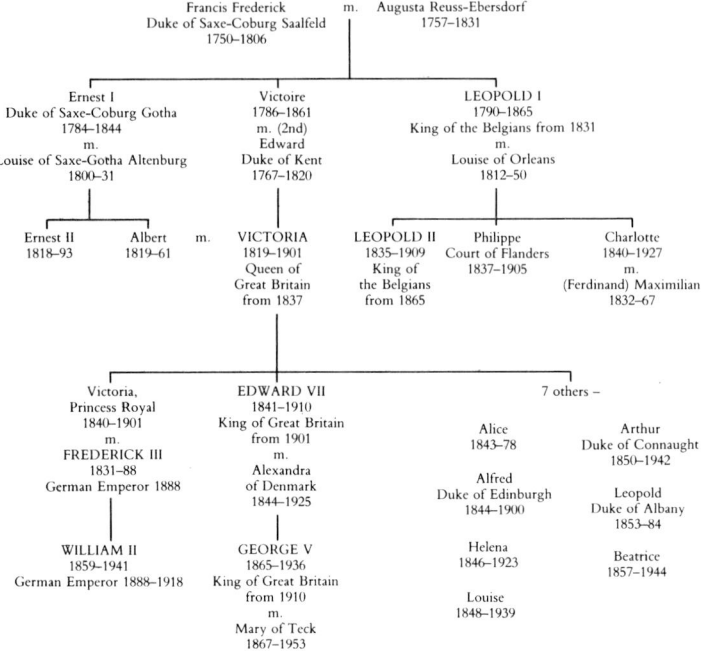

Francis Frederick
Duke of Saxe-Coburg Saalfeld
1750–1806

m.

Augusta Reuss-Ebersdorf
1757–1831

Ernest I
Duke of Saxe-Coburg Gotha
1784–1844
m.
Louise of Saxe-Gotha Altenburg
1800–31

Victoire
1786–1861
m. (2nd)
Edward
Duke of Kent
1767–1820

LEOPOLD I
1790–1865
King of the Belgians from 1831
m.
Louise of Orleans
1812–50

Ernest II
1818–93

Albert
1819–61

m.

VICTORIA
1819–1901
Queen of
Great Britain
from 1837

LEOPOLD II
1835–1909
King of
the Belgians
from 1865

Philippe
Court of Flanders
1837–1905

Charlotte
1840–1927
m.
(Ferdinand) Maximilian
1832–67

Victoria,
Princess Royal
1840–1901
m.
FREDERICK III
1831–88
German Emperor 1888

EDWARD VII
1841–1910
King of Great Britain
from 1901
m.
Alexandra
of Denmark
1844–1925

7 others –

Alice
1843–78

Alfred
Duke of Edinburgh
1844–1900

Helena
1846–1923

Louise
1848–1939

Arthur
Duke of Connaught
1850–1942

Leopold
Duke of Albany
1853–84

Beatrice
1857–1944

WILLIAM II
1859–1941
German Emperor 1888–1918

GEORGE V
1865–1936
King of Great Britain
from 1910
m.
Mary of Teck
1867–1953

Tables on this page and next are not complete. In the interests of clarity, most names not mentioned in the text of this book have been omitted.

The House of Habsburg-Lorraine

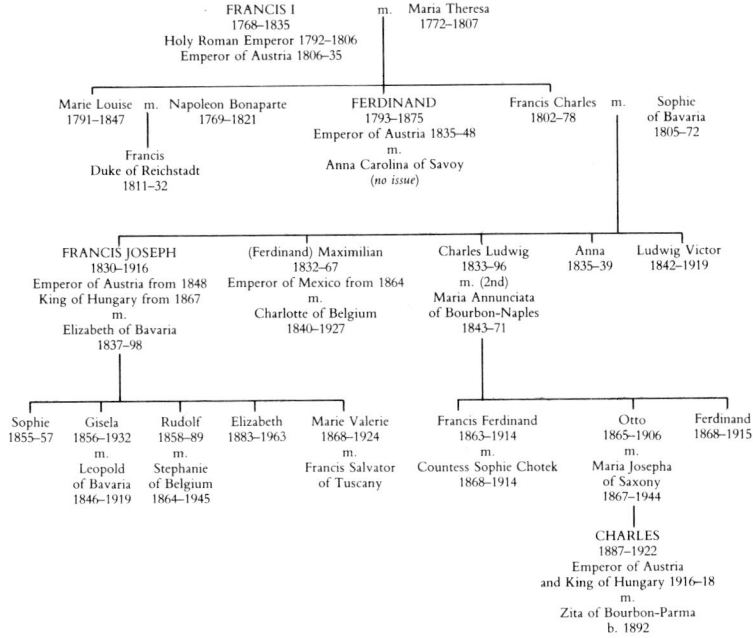

FRANCIS I
1768–1835
Holy Roman Emperor 1792–1806
Emperor of Austria 1806–35
m. Maria Theresa
1772–1807

Marie Louise
1791–1847
m. Napoleon Bonaparte
1769–1821

Francis
Duke of Reichstadt
1811–32

FERDINAND
1793–1875
Emperor of Austria 1835–48
m.
Anna Carolina of Savoy
(no issue)

Francis Charles
1802–78
m.
Sophie
of Bavaria
1805–72

FRANCIS JOSEPH
1830–1916
Emperor of Austria from 1848
King of Hungary from 1867
m.
Elizabeth of Bavaria
1837–98

(Ferdinand) Maximilian
1832–67
Emperor of Mexico from 1864
m.
Charlotte of Belgium
1840–1927

Charles Ludwig
1833–96
m. (2nd)
Maria Annunciata
of Bourbon-Naples
1843–71

Anna
1835–39

Ludwig Victor
1842–1919

Sophie
1855–57

Gisela
1856–1932
m.
Leopold
of Bavaria
1846–1919

Rudolf
1858–89
m.
Stephanie
of Belgium
1864–1945

Elizabeth
1883–1963

Marie Valerie
1868–1924
m.
Francis Salvator
of Tuscany

Francis Ferdinand
1863–1914
m.
Countess Sophie Chotek
1868–1914

Otto
1865–1906
m.
Maria Josepha
of Saxony
1867–1944

Ferdinand
1868–1915

CHARLES
1887–1922
Emperor of Austria
and King of Hungary 1916–18
m.
Zita of Bourbon-Parma
b. 1892

Prologue

In the first decade of the nineteenth century, while Europe was being torn apart by the Napoleonic wars, the Holy Roman Empire ceased to exist. The last emperor, Francis II, had long suspected Napoleon Bonaparte's intention of establishing a French-dominated empire throughout the continent, for with it would surely come the end of a balance of power which had existed since the tenth century – under Habsburg domination since 1273. Such a concept had increasingly become an anachronism, and in June 1806 Francis accordingly proclaimed himself Francis I, emperor of Austria. At the congress of Vienna in 1815, after the Napoleonic wars were over, the constituent territories of the Austrian empire were agreed. As well as present-day Austria and Hungary, they included Bohemia, Moravia, Galicia, Silesia, Slovakia, Transylvania, the Bukovina, Croatia-Slavonia, Carniola, Gorizia, Istria, Dalmatia, Lombardy and Venetia.

Though the Austrian empire comprised eleven nationalities, with a notable lack of geographic and economic unity, Austria herself emerged from the congress greatly enriched. The statesmen who had met in Vienna, particularly the Austrian foreign minister Prince Clemens von Metternich, had come with one common aim – to maintain the status quo of Europe. After twenty-three years fighting for their very existence, the powers were exhausted. It was a matter of vital importance that France should be kept under restraint, safely back behind her pre-revolutionary frontiers. The Austrian and Russian autocracies had survived, and Prussia had re-established herself on a more secure basis than formerly. The latter had been rewarded with Saxon territory and was given a commanding position on the Rhine, with the intention of preventing French expansion across the Northern Alps. Austria, with her Lombardy–Venetia possessions in Italy, likewise acted as an obstacle against French designs in the south. In addition, she assumed leadership of the confederation of German states.

This position was equally acceptable to the foreign policies of most European powers, not least Britain. To statesmen who governed during the thirty years or so after the battle of Waterloo, the most serious danger to continental stability was posed by the presence of two great aggressive military states on either side – France in the west,

Russia in the east. Between them lay a comparatively weak central area – a fragmented Germany, a multi-racial Austrian empire, and a divided Italy. It was in British interests to strengthen this area as the best means of maintaining order throughout Europe.

According to an entry in Queen Victoria's journal (1 January 1840), her prime minister Lord Melbourne maintained that Austria was 'the only country sincerely friendly to England'. Although Melbourne's remarks were often tinged with gentle irony and rarely meant to be taken at face value, in this case he personified something of the general British attitude towards the Habsburg domains. To all but an extreme radical minority, the idea of Europe without an Austrian empire, the reincarnation of the time-honoured Holy Roman empire, to preserve the balance of power, was unthinkable.

Respect for Austria from her fellow powers survived the death of Francis I in 1835 and the accession of his elder son Ferdinand. 'Ferdinand the Good-Natured' was mentally retarded and epileptic. With his ugly shrunken figure and enormous head, he could barely utter two connected sentences, lift a glass with one hand, or descend a staircase without assistance. He was one of the more pitiful examples of chronic Habsburg interbreeding. The blame for family deformities was placed on other factors which sound less credible today. Mental derangement and extreme ugliness in his sister Archduchess Marie was attributed to the fact that their mother had been chased during pregnancy by an orang-utang from the Schönbrunn zoo. Ferdinand's physicians permitted him to marry, though he suffered five epileptic attacks on the wedding night and it was undoubtedly beyond him to consummate the marriage. During his thirteen-year reign, all power remained firmly in the hands of Metternich.

It was therefore left to Ferdinand's younger brother, Archduke Francis Charles, to secure the imperial succession. In 1824 he had married Sophie, daughter of King Maximilian of Bavaria. Their first child, a son Francis (to which was later added the name Joseph) was born on 18 August 1830. During the next twelve years Sophie gave birth to three more sons – Ferdinand Maximilian, Charles Ludwig, and Ludwig Victor – as well as a sickly daughter Anna, who had inherited the Habsburg taint of epilepsy and died at the age of four.

To those who knew her well, the Archduchess Sophie was 'the only man in the Hofburg'.* Much as she admired Metternich as a politician, secretly agreeing with him that constitutions and democratic ideals were to be distrusted, she never forgave him for having allowed the feeble Ferdinand to ascend the throne instead of his brother. She knew that her mentally sound if uninspiring husband,

---

* The Hofburg and Schönbrunn palaces were the two principal imperial residences in Vienna, the former in winter and the latter in summer.

who was interested in nothing but sport and hunting, had no desire to assume the imperial burden. All her hopes and ambitions were centred on her eldest son. If she could not become an empress-consort herself, at least she could look forward to being the mother of an emperor.

In Vienna, economic unrest during the 1840s – poor harvests throughout Austria, mounting unemployment, and trading competition from Britain and Prussia – sowed the seeds of a depression which gradually spread from the poorer regions to more prosperous areas of the city. University students voiced the growing discontent, and on 12 March 1848 a petition was handed to the Emperor Ferdinand, demanding among other things dismissal of Metternich and his hated minister of police, Joseph Sedlnitsky. Early next day, a body of students marched on the Herrengasse. The army was sent out to curb the rioting and clear the streets, and in the ensuing fracas four men were killed. After a hasty conference at the Hofburg, where a garrison kept howling crowds at bay with some difficulty, it was agreed that the aged Metternich should be asked to resign. That evening he was summoned, and consented to his dismissal: 'I protest against calling my action a generous one. I act according to what I feel is right'. Two days later he left Vienna and fled for England.

Yet Metternich's departure was not enough for the crowds who demanded further reforms and continued to fight. Workers' and students' demonstrations, fuelled by sympathy for nationalist aspirations of those in the Italian territories and Hungary, made the atmosphere in Vienna so tense that the imperial family were compelled to move under cover of darkness to Innsbruck for several weeks. In October an army was assembled to fight the forces of Lajos Kossuth, the champion of Hungarian self-determination. The grenadiers refused to go, but joined the rioting crowds. During the street fighting which followed, Theodore Latour, minister of war, who had issued the orders for troops to leave for Hungary, was dragged from his office and lynched.

This was the climax of revolution in Vienna. The people gradually tired of months of anarchy and disorder, and at the end of October the city capitulated to the imperial troops. After another family conference, dominated by the Archduchess Sophie whose ambitions coincided perfectly with the plans of chief minister Prince Felix Schwarzenberg, Ferdinand was asked to abdicate. At such an unstable time, it was plainly unsuitable for the crown to be worn by one who was not merely unfitted to reign, but also hated by the people (through no fault of his own) as imperial personification of the system against which the Viennese had rebelled. After persuasion, Francis Charles renounced his place in the succession. The only possible new emperor, Sophie and Schwarzenberg declared, was her eldest son.

Untainted by association with the events of the last few months, he could serve as the symbol of a new era in the history of the Austrian empire.

On 2 December 1848, the family and ministers were bidden to appear before Emperor Ferdinand in the throne room. In his halting, at times barely coherent voice, he read a declaration to the effect that he was laying down the crown in favour of his beloved nephew.* At the age of eighteen, Archduke Francis (to whose baptismal name was now added that of Joseph after Joseph II, the much-revered reforming emperor), was proclaimed 'by God's grace' emperor of Austria, king of Jerusalem, apostolic king of Hungary, king of Bohemia, Galicia, Lodomeria, Lombardy, Venetia, Illyria and Croatia, archduke of Austria, and grand duke, duke, margrave, prince and count of some other thirty territories in the 35-million people-strong Austrian empire.

---

* After his abdication, Ferdinand was permitted to retain his title of emperor. He lived at Prague till his death in 1875, and was known affectionately as 'der Praguer Majestás', to distinguish him from his nephew. On his daily stroll along the ramparts, he would receive respectful salutes from the citizens.

CHAPTER 1

'He would risk anything'

On 18 December 1848 *The Times* informed its readers that

> In Austria the power and discipline of the army, directed with the skill of Generals and the moderation of statesmen, have saved the Empire. Francis Joseph I has mounted the throne of his fathers, stripped of no portion of his Imperial inheritance, and prepared, no doubt, with the advice of resolute Ministers, to convince his people, in the words of the late eloquent address to the Diet, that whenever the cause of progress is at stake the Imperial Government will take the lead in promoting it.

Though it is doubtful whether the significance crossed her mind, Queen Victoria and Emperor Francis Joseph had a common bond in the manner of their accessions. Both had succeeded aged uncles on the throne at the tender age of eighteen, and both were regarded optimistically by their ministers – if not their subjects as well – as marking the start of a new era. Nearly seventy years later, after both had died, it could be appreciated that each sovereign, by virtue of having the longest European reigns of the nineteenth and early twentieth centuries, had become uniquely loved and respected in their domains. In a sense the death of each, perhaps all the more poignant for occurring at a time of relative decline for their countries, signalled the end of an age.

Despite the absence of dynastic contacts and political ties between England and Austria during the nineteenth century, Queen Victoria and Prince Albert regarded themselves as pro-Austrian. Albert's cousin Count Alexander von Mensdorff, a son of the elder sister of the late Duke Ernest I of Saxe-Coburg Gotha, lived in Vienna, and both men enjoyed a lively correspondence.

It was only natural that Great Britain and Austria, as fellow-empires, should feel a kind of affinity. Not that either empire bore much resemblance to the other. At Queen Victoria's accession in 1837, the total area of the British empire outside the United Kingdom comprised over eight million square miles, with an estimated population of 96,000,000. By the time of her death, additional territories – notably from Africa and India – had resulted in an extra four million square miles of land and 124,000,000 more subjects, bringing the imperial population to over 360,000,000. Far removed from their imperial possessions, the British believed wholeheartedly that they were 'civilising the natives'. By contrast, the Habsburg empire was a huge, unwieldy bloc, united on paper as a mass of adjacent territories but in fact consisting of an anything but united assortment of racial groups. At the last imperial census in 1910, the population numbered nearly 50,000,000, with Austro-Germans (12,000,000) the largest group. All citizens of the Habsburg empire were white and European, even though they might only speak one of half a dozen different tongues. The British imperial crown prided itself as a common link presiding over its widely scattered dominions. The Catholic Habsburg crown, likewise the only link binding together its territories of which Austria occupied the geographical centre, regarded its status as the divinely-sanctioned guardian of unity and order, in theory if not in practice. After the other European powers' scramble for colonies in the late nineteenth century, Austria-Hungary was indeed the only purely European state of her standing in that she neither had nor desired colonies overseas.

Unfortunately for Queen Victoria and Prince Albert, and their relations with Austria, they were totally at odds with their foreign secretary where Europe was concerned. The irrepressible Henry John Temple, Viscount Palmerston, embodied a unique mixture of patriotism at home and radicalism abroad. When revolutionary fervour spread throughout the continent, it was inevitable that there would be clashes between crown and minister. Much as Victoria and Albert deprecated the cruelty of the Austrian rulers and native despots against their subjects, they were sympathetic to the Habsburgs as fellow-monarchs, and alarmed by the Italians' spirit of revolution, which could result in the suppression of many thrones whose occupants were entitled to their support. In some cases this went beyond mere solidarity between hereditary heads of state, for in the German confederation there were few kings or grand dukes who were not related by ties of blood or marriage.

The queen, eight months pregnant at the time, had been horrified by the revolution in France of February 1848 which resulted in the flight of the Orleans family to England. The aged ex-King Louis Philippe, clean-shaven and disguised in goggles and a cap, was smuggled across the English channel under the incognito of Mr Smith, to live out his remaining two years at Claremont in Surrey.

Only two weeks after Queen Victoria had given birth to her sixth child, Louise, came news that England had not escaped the forces of new radicalism after all. A large Chartist meeting, culminating in the presentation of a petition to Parliament, was to take place in London on 10 April, seven days hence. Extra police were hastily enrolled to maintain order, among them the adventurer Prince Louis Napoleon, destined to be president of the French republic within a year. In the end the meeting was an overwhelming failure. Only a few thousand demonstrators gathered instead of the expected half a million. The petition was presented, but as its 'signatures' included those of the duke of Wellington, Mr Punch and even Her Majesty Queen Victoria herself, Westminster was not alarmed.

As a young man Palmerston had been devoted to Italy and her desire for unity, and he spoke fluent Italian. While he could write with relief after the Chartist fiasco that the constables 'had sworn to make an example of any whiskered and bearded rioters whom they might meet with, and I am convinced they would have mashed them to jelly', he did not always side with law and order on the continent – at least not in the estimation of the royal and imperial houses of England and Austria. He believed in the maintenance of Habsburg rule, and lamented to Lord Ponsonby, ambassador in Vienna, that the qualities of intelligence, activity and energy could not 'be found in a Government where the sovereign is an idiot'. Even before Schwarzenberg and the Archduchess Sophie had done so, Palmerston was recommending that 'the idiot' should abdicate and his nephew ascend the throne in place of the Archduke Charles:

> . . .could not the son of that brother be called to the succession? And though he is young, he could yet mount his horse, and show himself to his troops and his people, could excite some enthusiasm for his person as well as for his official station, and, by the aid of good Ministers and able generals, might re-establish the Austrian empire in its proper position at home and abroad.[1]

Nobody could doubt his sincerity when he wrote to Ponsonby in June that, on behalf of the government, he recognised 'the importance of maintaining the Austrian empire as united and as strong as possible.'[2] Yet this concern did not overrule his eager partisanship of Italian rebels who wished to drive the Austrians, whose army under the octogenarian Field Marshal Radetsky was engaged in bringing them to heel, out of Venetia and Lombardy.

Queen Victoria found many of Palmerston's despatches to Ponsonby too strident in tone, and frequently returned them to be redrafted. In May she objected to one concerning alleged cruelties of Radetsky's forces at the village of Castelnuovo, which had been destroyed with considerable loss of civilian life. Pointing out that it was extremely difficult at a distance to judge acts committed during a war, that accounts were invariably exaggerated, and that she did not recall her government protesting after the governor of Venice's murder or any other treacherous acts committed by Italian rebels, she requested that the draft had 'better not be sent'. It would merely have the effect of unnecessarily irritating the Austrians, 'and increasing the distrust with which they view our sentiments on this question without doing any good'.[3] Palmerston graciously agreed to withhold the despatch, but his ebullient self-defence made it evident that he would not desist from his attitude.

After a series of Italian victories, Palmerston wrote (15 June) to Queen Victoria's uncle, King Leopold of the Belgians, that he could not but welcome the expulsion of the Austrians from Italy. Such an outcome would not

> diminish the real strength nor impair the real security of Austria as a European Power. Her rule was hateful to the Italians, and has long been maintained only by an expenditure of money and an exertion of military effort which left Austria less able to maintain her interests elsewhere. Italy was to her the heel of Achilles, and not the shield of Ajax. The Alps are her natural barrier and her best defence.[4]

In short, an Italy free from foreign control would no longer provide Austria – or France, or any other European power – with pretexts for expansion or interference which could result in war.

Yet Palmerston spoke too soon, for on 25 July Radetsky won a decisive victory against the Sardinian army at the battle of Custozza. Charles Albert, king of Sardinia, had no choice but to agree to an armistice.

On 11 November, Radetsky issued a proclamation on behalf of the government at Vienna announcing that he would not punish the Italian people who had been misled into rebelling against Austria, but merely the ringleaders – who would be ordered to pay heavy fines, amounting to confiscation of substantial parts of their estates and property. That many of these were drawn from the aristocratic classes was no accident, for the ministers hoped thus to pose as the champions of the lower classes against Italian nobility.

Palmerston was officially notified of the proclamation in advance, and wrote (14 November) to Ponsonby, asking him to urge the Austrian government not 'to imitate the most universally condemned excesses of the most desperate and unprincipled Revolutionists'.[5]

Three weeks later, Francis Joseph was on the throne. Schwarzenberg, newly appointed imperial chancellor and foreign minister, accordingly replied to Palmerston's retort, in the form of a private letter to the Austrian under-secretary for foreign affairs, with instructions to show it to Ponsonby. Schwarzenberg remarked that Palmerston was too inclined to consider himself the arbiter of Europe's destiny, and he for one would no longer tolerate 'his eternal insinuations, his tone now protective and pedantic, now insulting, but always unbecoming'. Did Lord Palmerston liken himself to King Louis XIV of France, he asked, and consider that *l'Angleterre c'est lui?*

As a final gesture, and one which would undoubtedly embarrass the foreign minister, no Habsburg archduke would be sent to the court at St James to announce the new emperor's accession. Schwarzenberg was not prepared to expose a prince to contact 'with the devoted protector of the Emperor's rebellious subjects'. Ponsonby forwarded a copy of the letter to Palmerston, who replied contemptuously that it was like 'the outpourings of an enraged woman of the town when arrested by a policeman in the act of picking a pocket'. Nonetheless he was concerned that nobody else should see the letter, and ordered that all copies should be removed from the embassy files and destroyed.

Much as Queen Victoria and Prince Albert deplored Palmerston's behaviour, the omission of an Austrian representative was a slight they felt deeply. Summoned by Prince Albert and blamed for this affront to Her Majesty, the minister was unrepentant. The snub, he answered, was to be taken as a compliment, since it came from a despotic government.

Later that month Prince Albert asked King Leopold to express his and the queen's sympathy to the Austrian court, and their strongest deprecation of 'this heartless, obstinate and revengeful man' Palmerston's Italian policy. Such a course of action might have been regarded as an indiscreet one for a constitutional monarch to take, and had the news leaked out it would have given weight to Palmerston's frequent complaints that Victoria and Albert considered foreign affairs their personal province on account of their family connections with European courts. Nonetheless Albert firmly believed that any contribution he could make personally to the maintenance of friendly relations with foreign courts was justified, and no harm was done.

Albert's wisdom in using his uncle as an intermediary with the Hofburg was soon justified, for early in the new year of 1849 one of Palmerston's most flagrant indiscretions came to light.

It was revealed by *The Times* that he had secretly supplied a British contractor with arms from the War Office for Sicilian rebels in November 1848, thus helping them in their fighting against Austria's close ally King Ferdinand of Naples, without openly infringing Britain's pledge of neutrality. Lord John Russell, the embarrassed prime minister, was summoned to Windsor on 24 January. Queen Victoria and Prince Albert were beside themselves with anger. It was intolerable, they told him, for England to have to apologise repeatedly for actions which her foreign minister had regularly taken without consulting anyone, and almost invariably in defiance of and counter to the wishes of the sovereign. Russell defended Palmerston as best he could, but drew the line at consenting to his dismissal. Under pressure Palmerston drafted a suitable apology, after initially declining to do so on the grounds that the king of Naples had not formally requested one.

Yet such events had not augured for good relations with the Austria of Emperor Francis Joseph at the start of his reign – good relations which Queen Victoria and Prince Albert viewed as essential for the stability and peaceful co-existence of Europe. It would not be the last time that the name of Palmerston was to incur the wrath of Austria.

The new emperor of Austria was a tall, slim young man, already – according to close observers at court – looking older than his eighteen years. As befitted a sovereign, he was proud of his skill as a horseman, and kept his military figure by regular riding, fencing, swimming and dancing. In early boyhood he had collected hand-painted toy soldiers, representing every Austrian regiment. It was a sign of efficiency beyond his tender age that he apparently never lost nor broke one. At the age of thirteen he was appointed colonel of a regiment of dragoons, which henceforth remained 'his dragoons'. In his periods of study (increased in his ninth year from thirteen to thirty-seven hours a week, and later to fifty) he was taught Italian, Czech, Hungarian, French, drawing, chemistry and political history. Music and literature bored him. The year after his accession, he described a festival commemorating the birth of Goethe as 'useless'. The empire, he believed, had 'better things and people to celebrate'. English was a significant omission from his education. It was one he later had cause to regret, for it meant he could only communicate with American officials through interpreters.*

In 1850, Schwarzenberg praised Francis Joseph for his acute intelligence and devotion to duty:

> He works hard for at least ten hours a day, and nobody knows better than I how many ministerial proposals he sends back to be revised. His bearing is full of dignity, his behaviour to all exceedingly polite, though a little dry. Men of sentiment – and many people in Vienna lay claim to kindliness – say that he has not much heart. There is no trace in him of that warm, superficial goodheartedness of many Archdukes, of the wish to please, to

---

* According to his biographer Margutti, most American officials in Vienna 'could not speak any other language'. He thus implies that their British counterparts in Austria were fluent to some degree in German, and therefore that the emperor's personal dealings with British staff were not handicapped by his linguistic shortcomings in the same way.

strive for effect. On the other hand he is perfectly accessible, patient and well disposed to be just to all. . .[6]

Like many European crowned heads who began to reign at an early age, Francis Joseph gave the impression of being more sure of himself than his sensitive youth really felt. This was well illustrated by an incident on the parade ground during the first few months of his rule, when what might have appeared to the casual onlooker an act of petty tyranny was no more than a manifestation of a young head of state keeping his subjects at arm's length. A senior general, many years older than the emperor himself, made a slight variation during military manoeuvres on imperial orders. The emperor called him up in front of the whole staff and ordered him to repeat the exercise as originally instructed: 'I command to be obeyed!'

The young man, who was said to have implored his uncle and parents after being called to his inheritance, 'Must I do without my youth?' had an awesome burden to support. This was not only on account of the vast territories over which he reigned, if not yet fully ruled.

As the successor of the Holy Roman emperors and sovereign of one of the foremost European powers, he was the most powerful figure in the continent, if not the world. Only Tsar Nicholas I of Russia could rival him in terms of imperial prestige. No other ruler could run him close. King Frederick William IV of Prussia was the weak-minded ruler of a kingdom whose potential was not to be realised for another two decades or so; Napoleon III, emperor of the French, was in the process of restoring his much-feared and least stable of countries from a republic to an empire, and regarded by his fellow-monarchs as an unprincipled *parvenu*; while Queen Victoria, who represented one of the most secure yet least powerful, least autocratic monarchies of the western world, was severely limited by virtue of her parliament and constitution.

In 1851 Francis Joseph approved the creation of an advisory parliament of sorts, but it was more of a token experiment in democracy than a body of constitutionally-recognised means. It was, he announced, to 'fortify in every respect the moral principle of imperial authority and to widen the limits of a power which had proved itself useful for centuries'. By the end of the year, encouraged no doubt by the example of Louis Napoleon in France, this brief exercise in democracy had been placed in abeyance. According to Francis Joseph, ministers could only be responsible to the monarch, therefore the constitutional principle of England (if not France as well) could not be applied to the Austrian state; 'irresponsible sovereignty' was 'a phrase without meaning'.

The young emperor's earnestness of purpose was not looked on approvingly in all corners of Europe. Queen Victoria noted a conversation in her journal (13 January) with General Radowitz, foreign minister of Prussia, who told her that he was

> serious, clever, distinguished, very well educated, and with a great knowledge of languages and military affairs. He was very determined, possessed of an iron will, so that he would risk anything, to carry through what he once considered to be right. This, I think is rather a misfortune.[7]

No less a misfortune for some occurred in September 1850, when the Austrian General Julius Haynau paid a private visit to England. Nicknamed 'General Hyaena' after his brutal suppression of Italian and Hungarian men, women and children, he attempted to visit Barclay & Perkins' brewery at Southwark. The indignant radical press, warned of his imminent appearance, had published an extraordinarily lifelike cartoon of the bushy-browed, luxuriantly-moustachioed tyrant flogging a woman. On his arrival at the brewery he was instantly recognised. One furious drayman grabbed him and tried to shave him on the premises, another dropped a bale of straw on his head, and in the course of matters his clothes were torn. Fighting his way into the street he was pulled along by his moustache, and had to be rescued from his unrepentant attackers by police.

Queen Victoria was horrified that a foreign dignitary should be treated to such an unbecoming reception in her kingdom. At first she thought that the guilty party must have been Hungarian refugees. When she discovered that British workmen were responsible, she asked Palmerston to express the government's deep regret at the 'brutal outrage on one of the Emperor's distinguished generals and subjects'. Palmerston did, but he was too honest to conceal the delight he shared with the majority of Britons. In his official despatch for Ponsonby to present Schwarzenberg, he regretted the attack but added in his final paragraph that it had been extremely ill-advised for Haynau to visit England in view of the popular indignation felt for him throughout the country. It would be injudicious, he went on, for the Austrian government to press for a prosecution against the draymen, because at any trial Haynau's atrocities in Italy and Hungary would certainly be referred to by the defence counsel.

Palmerston showed the draft to Her Majesty, who insisted that all criticisms of the general's visit should be deleted. When he informed her that the despatch had already gone to Vienna, she was furious. She ordered him to send a second one cancelling the first, and omitting the offending paragraph. Palmerston appealed to Russell, declaring that if an altered despatch was to be sent, then it would have to be signed by a new secretary of state for foreign affairs – in short, he would resign. The prime minister proved adamant, Palmerston discreetly withdrew his threat, and eventually Vienna – by now doubtless used to the antics of this outspoken minister across the North Sea – received the desired apology.

The court were secretly relieved that Palmerston did not resign after all over the issue, especially since a letter from Mensdorff in Vienna (14 October) to Albert confirmed their suspicions regarding Haynau; he was 'a thoroughly bad character and richly deserves what he got'. It fully endorsed Palmerston's self-defence that the general's behaviour had aroused almost as much disgust in Austria as in England, and that the epithet of 'Hyaena' had originally been bestowed on him in Vienna.

It was appropriate that the great exhibition of 1851 in Hyde Park, London, the crowning achievement of Prince Albert's life – and, perhaps, of Victorian England – should have provided an opportunity for the first exchange of correspondence between Queen Victoria and the Emperor Francis Joseph.

Not the least of Albert's problems in organising the exhibition was the attitude of continental rulers. Though they were happy enough to see their countries represented among the exhibits, after their initial interest in the opening ceremony they had second thoughts. After surviving the revolutions of 1848 with thrones if not autocratic powers intact, they had no desire to meet an untimely end from terrorists in a foreign land whose hospitality to refugees from other countries was legendary. Few might have agreed wholeheartedly with a spiteful letter from King Ernest Augustus of Hanover, who had long nursed a personal grudge against his niece Queen Victoria and even more so against her husband, that 'this rubbishy Exhibition' was causing the government anxiety because of 'the infamies, plots and *menées* of the excommunicated in all lands, who are now in London'.[8] Yet they could not help feeling that there was an element of truth in this, and it took all Albert's powers of persuasion to change the mind of King Frederick William IV, fearful of losing one of his few allies, and allow his brother William and family to represent Prussia at the opening ceremony on 1 May.

Bearing in mind Francis Joseph's lack of interest in arts and commerce, and in view of Palmerston's effect on Anglo-Austrian relations, it is unlikely that he ever considered travelling to Hyde Park for the purpose, or even sending an archduke to represent him. Yet he sent several exhibits, among them a magnificent oak cabinet of intricate Gothic design carved by Leistler of Vienna. A personal gift to the sovereign, after the exhibition closed in October it was installed in one of Prince Albert's workrooms at Buckingham Palace.*

* It was later presented to the university of Edinburgh by King George V.

The cabinet was accompanied by a friendly, if of necessity formal and brief, letter (19 April):

> I cannot deny myself the pleasure of taking advantage of the occasion offered to me by the exhibition of industry which is about to open under the auspices of Your Majesty, of paying homage to you by sending an example of the industry of my empire.
>
> Destined as it is for your personal use, this object will, I hope, sometimes assist you in recalling the feelings of sincere friendship which I pledge to you. . .[9]

The queen replied in kind (5 May):

> I hasten to thank Your Imperial Majesty for the excellent examples of industry and the arts of Your Empire which you have been so kind to send and which we treasure, firstly as they come from Your Majesty and then because of their great beauty, and also as souvenirs of the age in which it has pleased the Almighty to allow such a peaceable gathering of all nations of the world and their products. – The ceremony of the opening of the Exhibition has made the greatest impression on my heart and I was sorry to have been the only Sovereign to enjoy such an imposing and moving scene. We have already made several visits to the Austrian section and the Prince and I have had occasion to admire greatly the products which have come from your empire. May their exhibition contribute to the prosperity and commerce of the Austrian empire.
>
> Please accept this expression of my sincere friendship which I hope will one day be cemented by the personal acquaintance of Your Majesty. . .[10]

Such a meeting was not destined to take place for some eleven years.

Unhappily, the close of the extremely successful exhibition in October 1851 coincided with another brush between England and Austria. A group of Hungarian and Polish refugees, led by Lajos Kossuth, came to England en route for America to express their thanks to Palmerston for his moral support in their struggle against Austria and Russia during the rising of 1848–49. When Kossuth arrived at Southampton, he was greeted with a reception and banquet by the mayor and corporation, and people turned out in their thousands to cheer him. In his speeches he fiercely denounced the absolutist governments of both empires. Queen Victoria railed bitterly against the 'stupid Kossuth fever'; and her ministers were alarmed when the *Morning Post* officially announced the Hungarian patriot's intention of calling on Palmerston to express his thanks for everything he had done for the refugees in Turkey. Russell protested, but Palmerston replied that he would not be dictated to as to whom he saw in his own house. Under the queen's threat to dismiss him if he persisted, the foreign secretary gave way again, earning a contemptuous rebuke from Prince Albert for clinging to office rather than standing by his principles. However, Palmerston got his own back two days later by receiving a deputation from the boroughs of Islington and Finsbury, congratulating him on his support for Kossuth in saving the oppressed Poles and Hungarians from the Austrian and Russian emperors, stigmatised as 'odious and detestable assassins', and 'merciless tyrants and despots'. Although the meeting was private, and in spite of Palmerston's speech of thanks in which he said he could not be expected to endorse the language they had used about the emperor and the tsar, a journalist was present and reported everything. It was widely felt that this action was worse than if he had simply received Kossuth instead.

It was thus to a background of rather strained relations that Queen Victoria presented the emperor with a gift of Staffordshire pottery which had been so admired at the exhibition (18 November):

> I must dare to ask if Your Imperial Majesty will kindly accept a little souvenir of the Universal Exhibition in which the industry of Your Majesty's lands has taken such a noble part. It is Staffordshire porcelain which I hope you will permit the manufacturer, Mr Minton, an excellent and worthy man, to lay at Your Majesty's feet in my name.
>
> I take this occasion to thank Your Majesty for the kind reception which you gave my aunt and cousin of Cambridge during their stay at Vienna and Ischl and I entreat you to believe in our unalterable friendship. . .[11]

To which the emperor replied (15 December):

> I hasten to offer Your Majesty my most grateful thanks for the magnificent present which you have entrusted Mr Minton to give me in your name. I shall treasure it as a souvenir of this friendship, so precious to me, of which I have to my great pleasure found new assurance in the letter which Your Majesty did me the honour of addressing me on 18 November. . .[12]

During the first thirteen years of her reign, Queen Victoria had experienced three attempts on her life. None, however, was as serious as that which almost brought Francis Joseph to an untimely death.

On 18 February 1853, he was taking a midday stroll in Vienna, accompanied only by an adjutant, Maximilian O'Donnell. As he stepped on to a wall surrounding the inner city, to watch a regiment going through exercises on the other side, a young man sitting on a nearby bench drew a knife from his coat and threw himself on the emperor. A woman standing only feet away screamed, and he instinctively turned towards the noise. This reaction probably saved his life, for the would-be assassin's weapon slipped and merely wounded him in the neck. O'Donnell flung himself on the man, a Hungarian tailor's apprentice named Johann Libényi. Suffering from shock, Francis Joseph was taken to the palace of Archduke Albrecht, and the roads and railway stations of Vienna were temporarily blocked while authorities tried in vain to find evidence of a conspiracy.

The assassination attempt was widely discussed throughout Europe. 'How awful the outrage committed on the young Emperor is,' the prince of Prussia wrote to Bismarck, while in a letter to the same prince, Prince Albert saw it as part of a malaise affecting the Austrian empire as a result of her Italian policy:

> How tragic the recent executions and oppressions throughout Northern Italy, justified though they are by necessity. And above all how tragic the murderous attempt on the life of the poor young Emperor. All this is bound to leave behind it a deep impression in Austria, and make it more and more uncertain how the tottering Imperial State may produce law and order out of this alternation of criminal excesses and drastic repressions.[13]

Shouting '*Eljen Kossuth!*' ('Long live Kossuth!'), Libényi was dragged away by police and executed within a fortnight. During this time the emperor's wound bled severely and he suffered a partial temporary loss of eyesight. As late as 6 March, Queen Victoria noted in her journal that 'though he may to all appearances seem well, he might die suddenly at any moment'.[14] On 17 March, by which time he was pronounced out of danger, came a revelation which had its comic side. Again, from the queen's journal:

> The absurdities believed abroad, but principally at Vienna, are such, that one can hardly credit them. Amongst others is the following: on the knife with which the Emperor was stabbed, and on those used in Milan, which were of Birmingham manufacture, it was found that they were stamped "Palmer And Son", upon which people declared it was "Palmerston", and that Lord Palmerston had had them made on purpose!![15]

Though the Viennese cannot have been aware of it at the time, Palmerston's name was about to be linked with Austria once more as a result of an unfortunate coincidence. Shortly after his reception of the pro-Kossuth demonstration in 1851, he had at last overstepped his limits by welcoming the *coup d'état* of Louis Napoleon in Paris, and had been dismissed from office. Within weeks he had helped bring down the government, joined a Whig–Peelite coalition with Lord Aberdeen as prime minister, and returned to office as home secretary.

In April 1853, while Francis Joseph was still recovering from Libényi's attempt on his life, Palmerston was informed by the chief commissioner of the metropolitan police, Sir Richard Mayne, of a conspiracy. Kossuth, then living in Manchester, had befriended Mr Hain, an arms manufacturer of radical sympathies. Between them, they were apparently engaged in the process of plotting to produce and export arms to Hungary, where rebel forces would use them to expel the Austrians. Under Palmerston's authority, Mayne applied for a warrant to search Hain's premises in Rotherhithe, and found an arsenal of rockets and gunpowder far exceeding the quantity which an arms manufacturer was permitted to store without a licence. Hain was accordingly charged with an offence under the explosives act.

The Times revealed this news with more enthusiasm than accuracy. No mention was made of Hain at first, and an indignant public was led to believe that Kossuth was secretly making arms himself in a house in Rotherhithe. Radicals fiercely denounced the paper for its campaign against him, suggesting that it was seizing any pretext for stirring popular opinion up against refugees and foreign revolutionary exiles in Britain, and maintaining that Austrian agents were responsible for police harassing refugees.

John Bright, then Liberal member for Manchester, questioned Palmerston in the House of Commons, asking him to state categorically that Kossuth had no connection with the arsenal. Palmerston refused to do so, but admitted that as home secretary he accepted full responsibility for the police action. He mentioned that Austrian authorities had recently been alarmed by importation of knives marked Palmer & Son, especially in view of the recent attack on the emperor, and it would not be conducive to relations between both countries by allowing more arms to be sent from London to Hungary. His evasive replies to further questions in the House could not disguise the fact that plain-clothes policemen had been employed by the government for some years to watch political refugees and others. Obviously a person of Kossuth's reputation could not be excluded from such surveillance.

As home secretary, Palmerston thus made it abundantly clear that he was more interested in the prevention of crime than in remaining the radicals' hero. This did not escape the notice of Queen Victoria and Prince Albert, who nursed secret hopes that their *bête noire* was at last growing old gracefully.

'Austria is the keystone of European policy', King Leopold of the Belgians once declared; 'its existence is essential to the European equilibrium.' It was therefore from the Habsburgs that he sought a bride for his elder son Leopold, duke of Brabant. In the spring of 1853, a betrothal was announced between Prince Leopold and Archduchess Marie Henriette, daughter of Archduke Joseph of Tuscany. King Leopold felt his dynasty would be strengthened by an alliance with the Habsburgs, and he was much impressed by what he saw of the Viennese court, as well as by its sovereign. To Queen Victoria he wrote (3 June), praising Francis Joseph warmly:

> There is much sense and courage in his warm blue eye [*sic*], and it is not without a very amiable merriment when there is occasion for it. He is slight and very grateful, but even in the *melée* of dancers and Archdukes, and all in uniform, he may always be distinguished as the *Chief*.[16]

The queen's lack of enthusiasm for the match pained King Leopold – 'about what is to be done by way of graciousness on your part we will consider' – and he was prepared for political hostility:

> I trust that this family connection may mitigate the only impression which in Austria has created a hostile feeling, viz. the suspicions in Palmerston's time that it had become a plan of England *to destroy* the Austrian Empire.[17]

Nothing was to be allowed to lessen King Leopold's sense of triumph at this marriage alliance. In his self-congratulatory manner he attached no significance to the fact that his lugubrious, unprepossessing son and the attractive, lively archduchess took an instant dislike to each other. Within four years the king's only daughter would make a scarcely more happy marriage with the Habsburgs, and the second daughter of his son and the archduchess would establish a third matrimonial bond between the Coburgs and the imperial dynasty – one which would end in a tragedy almost unparalleled in the annals of nineteenth-century royalty.

During 1853 the great powers slowly but surely drifted into war. For years, Russian ambitions at the expense of the Turkish empire had made Europe uneasy. Matters came to a head when Tsar Nicholas I claimed that followers of the Russian Orthodox faith in the Ottoman empire were being persecuted, and demanded 'proper satisfaction from the Turkish government'. European rulers were not taken in. What Russia really wanted was expansion, and she was prepared to achieve it by force. In particular she coveted the Dardanelles which would guarantee her free passage from the Black Sea to the Mediterranean. Russia would therefore be a major power in the western world, a rival of Austria and her polyglot empire if not also a threat to her in the Balkans, and a competitor for England's maritime powers. England had a vested interest in seeing Constantinople free from Russian interference.

The tsar demanded to know from Francis Joseph whether Austria would support Russia in her proposed action against the sultan, whom he called 'the sick man on the Bosphorus', reminding him of his debt of gratitude to the ruler who had helped suppress the Hungarians. The young Austrian emperor was caught in a difficult position. Nicholas, he knew, was hated throughout Europe as the ruthless autocrat who had maintained serfdom, destroyed Polish liberties, and acted with what had been considered unnecessary cruelty in Hungary. Nowhere was this opinion held more strongly than in England and France, who were powerful albeit geographically remote powers in western Europe whom it was important not to offend, especially France who could easily ferment trouble in Austria's Italian territories. However, he recognised that he was eternally in the tsar's debt. To side with England and France on the one hand, or with Russia on the other, could precipitate a return to the anarchy of 1848 that had plunged Europe into disarray. The last thing the twenty-two-year-old autocrat wished to do was to risk unleashing forces that might well sweep his empire into oblivion.

Before his evasive letter to Nicholas counselling caution was received, the latter had claimed a Russian protectorate over Christians living in the Ottoman empire. Turkey indignantly rejected the ultimatum. At the end of May, Russian troops prepared to attack Turkey; meanwhile the tsar suggested to Francis Joseph that Austrian soldiers ought to occupy (in other words, annex) Bosnia and Herzegovina, so that both of their 'great countries' would ultimately gain sovereignty over all the Slav races.

Queen Victoria, Prince Albert, the British government, and public opinion alike were united in outright condemnation of such behaviour. Lord Aberdeen, who was mildly sympathetic to Russia and seemed almost alone in Britain in his belief that her intentions were not totally dishonourable, believed so strongly that peace could be preserved through negotiation that he initially countermanded an order for the British fleet to be sent to the Dardanelles so as to assist the Turks in protecting their coast against Russian ships, and objected to a proposal that if Russia invaded the principalities of Moldavia and Wallachia, Britain would declare war. Palmerston and Russell, who reflected popular opinion in their support of Turkey and their suspicion of Russian designs on the British trade route to India, argued strongly against him. By the time the British cabinet was united in agreeing to send the fleet, Russia had invaded.

Francis Joseph attempted in vain to mediate between the tsar and the sultan. Meetings between the emperor, tsar and King Frederick William IV of Prussia also failed, and in October Russia declared war on Turkey. Despite the tsar's persistent bullying, Francis Joseph preserved Austrian neutrality, even after Britain and France declared war on Russia early in 1854. In May he ordered troops to Galicia to prevent the possibility of Russian invasion, and demanded the withdrawal of Russia from the Danube principalities. In December 1854, largely at the insistence of his foreign minister Count Buol, he signed an agreement with Britain and France which demanded Russia's abandonment of any claims over the sultan's Christian subjects, and reversion of rights over the Dardanelles in favour of the western allies.

In view of the inept, disease-ridden campaigns pursued at the Crimea, it was perhaps fortunate for Austria in the short run that her forces remained out of the fighting. Nonetheless the price paid by Francis Joseph was high. Tsar Nicholas died suddenly in March 1855. Some said it was by his own hand, unable to entertain the shame of defeat; others, including his son who ascended the imperial throne as Tsar Alexander II, claimed it was of a broken heart at Austrian ingratitude. In Britain (where Lord Palmerston had succeeded Aberdeen as prime minister) and France, hopes had been entertained that Austria would join the western allies and help defeat Russia more quickly. In Prussia, King Frederick William and his ministers had felt betrayed that their ally in the German confederation should abandon his neutrality and sign the agreement without consulting them.

In January 1856 Francis Joseph sent Russia an ultimatum, and a peace conference met at Paris the following month. That Austria should take it upon herself to act as mediator and help negotiate peace terms was generally resented. Most members of the German confederation were critical of his ingratitude to an old and valued friend. He was regarded more sympathetically in Britain, though Sir Hamilton Seymour, ambassador to St Petersburg, recognised that 'there was no doubt' the young emperor 'felt his isolation deeply'.

By this time Francis Joseph's isolation had begun not only in a political sense, but also on a personal level.

The Archduchess Sophie had redoubled her efforts to find a daughter-in-law after the attempt on his life in 1853. Although he had three younger brothers, the dynasty had to be perpetuated into the next generation. Princesses who were Catholics or prepared to embrace the Catholic faith for the honour of becoming empress of Austria were few, and in the end she narrowed the choice down to her niece Helene. The daughter of Sophie's younger sister Ludovika and the eccentric Duke Max in Bavaria, Helene was a well-educated, serious girl of eighteen when Sophie arranged a family rendezvous at Ischl in August 1853. But the carefully-planned match was not to be. Francis Joseph only had eyes for her younger sister Elizabeth, an enchantingly pretty fifteen-year-old. For the first and perhaps the last time in his life the emperor defied his mother. He would marry Elizabeth or nobody.

The whirlwind courtship and marriage of these two young people was one which they would later have good cause to regret. No woman of noble birth was ever less fitted to become an empress. Elizabeth had inherited her father's love of horses and his gipsy temperament, and as a circus performer or lady of leisure responsible only for a large stable of horses she would have been in her element. But she had been poorly-educated, let alone prepared for such a destiny, and she was pathologically shy.

Long before the wedding at Vienna in April 1854, Sophie recognised that the girl must be groomed carefully as befitted the first lady of the mighty Austrian Empire. Her domineering character repelled Elizabeth, whose initial dislike hardened rapidly into lasting resentment. When she gave birth to a daughter in March 1855, her name Sophie chosen naturally by the proud grandmother, the baby was taken and brought up in a nursery next to the archduchess's suite in the Hofburg. If Elizabeth wanted to see her child, she had to climb a long staircase and walk through several passages. When she arrived, the grandmother was nearly always present, like a sentry on guard duty.

Francis Joseph remained in love with her until her tragic death forty-four years later. Yet he was first and foremost an emperor wielding power and occupying a pre-eminence among crowned heads well beyond his age and experience, only second (and a poor second at that) a husband and family man. It was unfortunate that the first year of his married life had to coincide with the Crimean war and his agonising over how to conduct Austria's position *vis-à-vis* the other powers.

But even if he had not had to fend off Tsar Nicholas in the weeks before and after his wedding, it is doubtful whether he and Elizabeth would have made a greater success of their life together. For all his love of her, he was too clumsy and not understanding enough. Like him, she was too emotionally immature; moreover, she was a painfully inexperienced sixteen and like nearly all young brides of the age totally innocent of the facts of life. A gentler, more tactful husband might have broken down the reserve and helped her to adjust from an unfettered girlish upbringing to her new existence as an empress in a court famed for its tedious formality. For all his sober virtues, Francis Joseph was not the man. The price he was about to pay, in terms of emotional and personal isolation, was a heavy one.

CHAPTER 2

'A remarkable young man'

During the first eight years of Francis Joseph's reign, Queen Victoria never met any members of the Habsburg family. Such lack of personal contact invariably tended to reinforce any prejudices she might have had about them and indeed about Austria generally, fostered if not inspired by hearsay. Any suspicions or dislike she may have felt about European rulers or princes were usually dispelled the moment she met them. As a young spinster queen she had dreaded a visit from the Tsarevich Alexander (now Tsar Alexander II), but after entertaining him to a round of theatres and concerts in London and dancing in his arms, she 'felt so sad to take leave of this dear amiable young man whom I really think (talking jokingly) I was a little in love with'. Napoleon III was 'an extraordinary man' with whom one could 'never be for one instant safe' after his seizure of power in 1851 (it may be safely assumed that she was referring to his political ambitions, rather than to any over-zealous personal habits). Four years later, on his state visit to England, she was fascinated beyond measure by his 'quiet, frank manner'.

Would the young emperor of Austria, who never set foot once on British soil during his eighty-six years, have charmed Her Majesty in like fashion, if they had met in similar circumstances during the 1850s, before widowhood cast its overwhelming shadow over the court at Windsor?

In view of his straightforward, earnest manner, his habit of keeping others at arm's length, and his tortuous relationship with Elizabeth, it seems unlikely. More telling, perhaps, is the impression his brother, still his heir, who differed from him so much, was to make on Queen Victoria.

Ferdinand Maximilian was born on 6 July 1832, twenty-three months his eldest brother's junior. According to gossip, his father was probably Napoleon Bonaparte's sickly, tubercular son the duke of Reichstadt. The Archduchess Sophie had always been closer to this sensitive artistic young Frenchman, who lived in Vienna, than to her mediocre husband. Max, as he was known in the family, grew up to be his mother's favourite, and much more like the Wittelsbachs on his mother's side, even more like the invalid French duke, who died when he was sixteen days old, than the Archduke Francis Charles. While Francis Joseph was a model Habsburg, unimaginative, uninterested in the arts, yet efficient and dedicated, Max was sensitive, intellectual, and a dreamer.

If he could be the most charming of the four brothers he was also the naughtiest and laziest, given to moods of radiant happiness one moment, depression or tantrums the next. When their only sister Anna died, Francis Joseph consoled their mother with a solicitude which belied his ten years of age. Max's reaction was to spend a month's pocket money on buying her a pet monkey, regretting tenderly as he presented it to her that he could not purchase another little girl instead.

The two brothers were always close during boyhood, and one day played a prank on the family which belies the belief that Habsburgs had no sense of humour. Max dressed in women's clothes and got Francis Joseph to introduce him at court as a Princess of Modena, cousin to the empress. The latter was fascinated by this supposed new relation, and wondered why they had not met before. Then the 'princess' unwittingly emitted a most unladylike belch.

As a young man Max joined the Austrian navy; in 1854 he was promoted to rear-admiral, and appointed commander-in-chief. His service duties took him regularly to Vienna and Trieste. He thus had the chance to see at close range the results of Radetsky's repression in Venetia and Lombardy which were bringing Austria a reputation for cruelty among liberals throughout Europe – among which he was inclined to number himself. He was disgusted at the way in which Tsar Nicholas had assisted Austria in crushing Hungarian freedom. Because of his pride in naval matters, he admired Britain and her navy, and he would have liked to take part, as a British ally, in naval engagements against the Russians in the Crimea. Not the least interesting of nineteenth-century hypothetical questions is speculation as to how Austria would have fared under her Emperor Ferdinand Maximilian, if Libényi's knife had found its target that day in February 1853.

At the age of twenty, Max fell in love with and became betrothed to Princess Maria Amalia, daughter of the ex-emperor of Brazil. This match was regarded with scant approval at Vienna, and it was agreed that the engagement should not be announced until Max attained his majority. By that time the princess had succumbed to consumption, and he was shattered by the loss.

In the summer of 1856, Queen Victoria and King Leopold of the Belgians were much concerned over marital prospects for Leopold's daughter Charlotte. Initially she had two suitors, Prince George of

Saxony, and her cousin King Pedro V of Portugal. She was unimpressed by George, and she dreaded the prospect of having to make her home in Lisbon. While she and her father weighed over the respective merits of each, Max arrived in Brussels. The Archduchess Sophie had decided that the time was right for her second son to settle down, and among marriageable Catholic princesses the intelligent and attractive Charlotte of Belgium figured strongly. For his part, the ambitious Leopold, who had raised the newly-founded little kingdom to the rank of a model democratic European power, believed that further dynastic ties with Austria would be valuable in securing an ally against possible French aggression and expansion which threatened to absorb Belgium. At Vienna, the prospect of a second Habsburg–Coburg marriage was regarded favourably as a prelude to closer relations with England.

The sixteen-year-old princess, who had been starved of affection since the age of ten by her mother's death and become serious and introspective beyond her years, found a kindred spirit in Max. Leopold refused to try and influence his daughter in her choice. Writing to Queen Victoria (10 October 1856), he admitted to preferring the prospect of Pedro as a son-in-law, but recognised that the archduke had made a favourable impression on her.

The queen was vehemently in favour of the young king of Portugal. She replied (13 October):

> . . .*I still hope* by your letter that Charlotte has not finally made up her mind – as we both feel so strongly convinced of the immense superiority of Pedro over any other young Prince. . .besides which the position is so infinitely preferable. The Austrian society is *médisante* and profligate and worthless – and the Italian possessions very shaky. . .[1]

But Charlotte had already decided on Max. He was strangely hesitant at first, writing in prosaic and anything-but-besotted terms to his younger brother Charles Ludwig that

> She is small, I am tall, which is as it should be. She is brunette and I am fair, which is also good. She is very clever, which is a bit worrying, but no doubt I will get over that.[2]

He was well aware of the Coburg reputation for ambition, and perhaps he recognised that a heavy responsibility would fall on any son-in-law of the crafty, dynastically-obsessed King Leopold. Nonetheless he was flattered by Charlotte's devotion and by the fact that she preferred him to Pedro and George. Moreover, he knew that his mother and brother expected him to marry and settle down, and in

Charlotte he might find the happiness of which he had been cruelly deprived by the sudden death of Maria Amalia. In October 1856 his proposal was accepted. Leopold, who had detected Max's hesitation and had heard certain indiscreet remarks, could not resist a little gentle teasing in welcoming him into the family:

> My dear and honoured friend appears to regard me as a wily diplomat, whose every move is dictated by politics. I assure you this is not the case. As long ago as last May, you succeeded in winning my confidence and esteem, irrespective of any other consideration. I soon noticed that my daughter was of the same opinion.[3]

The hopes of father and daughter that Max might find some promotion were soon realised, for shortly after the engagement he was raised to the rank of vice-admiral and appointed governor of Venetia–Lombardy. Francis Joseph had been advised that the oppressive military regime in his Italian provinces was a failure and that only more conciliatory management could prevent another revolution. It was not a move which pleased everybody, for Max's governorship did not include the military command. This was given to Count Gyulai, senior military officer in Italy, as a compromise designed not to offend the army who worshipped the once-mighty but now hopelessly senile Radetsky. Under the liberal-minded but sadly inexperienced Archduke Ferdinand Maximilian, the army would have been restless. With the reactionary Gyulai, who had scarcely any more sympathy for Italian nationalist aspirations than his predecessor, the forces would surely be more contented. Max accepted his emasculated post reluctantly, for he saw that the partnership between Gyulai and himself was unlikely to be a happy one. At the root of his problem was a feeling that the emperor merely wished him to be a figurehead with the minimum of responsibility.

Queen Victoria's sweeping comments about 'worthless Austrian archdukes' had made a considerable impact on King Leopold. However a visit from Charlotte did more to persuade her than all the letters from the palace at Laeken. The sixteen-year-old princess was no longer the withdrawn, brooding girl she had seemed since her mother's death, but radiantly transformed by the prospect of marriage.

The queen and Prince Albert needed little persuasion to invite Max, and on 30 May 1857 he set sail from Venice in the Austrian steam frigate *Elizabeth*. Escorted up the English channel by a fleet of destroyers and greeted with a 21-gun salute, the ship arrived at

Portsmouth on 15 June. After being welcomed on to English soil by the Austrian ambassador Count Apponyi, and the queen's equerry Lord Charles Fitzroy, Max travelled by train to Windsor.

This first meeting of Queen Victoria and Prince Albert with a member of the Habsburgs was an unqualified success, in personal terms at least. Max had long since warmed to the British way of life through his visits to units of the Mediterranean fleet. He was genuinely pleased to make the acquaintance of the royal family, in whom he found a sincere welcoming spirit and closeness which contrasted with the tense atmosphere of the Hofburg, dominated by an elder, faintly jealous and suspicious brother with whom he now had so little in common, and a mother and sister-in-law who were barely on speaking terms.

The whole British royal family had assembled for the christening of Queen Victoria's youngest child Beatrice, at the private chapel in Buckingham Palace, on 16 June. Also present was her future son-in-law Prince Frederick William ('Fritz') of Prussia, betrothed to Victoria ('Vicky'), Princess Royal. Max, Vicky and Fritz were among the baby princess's sponsors.

After the ceremony and luncheon in the ballroom, at which Queen Victoria sat between the two handsome young bridegrooms-to-be, she took back her earlier strictures and wrote glowingly to King Leopold that

> I cannot say how much we like the Archduke; he is charming, so clever, natural, kind, and amiable, so English in his feelings and likings, and so anxious for the best understanding between Austria and England. With the exception of his mouth and chin he is good-looking, but I think one does not in the least care for that, as he is so very kind, clever, and pleasant. I wish you really joy, dearest Uncle, as I am sure he is quite worthy of her, and will make her happy.
>
> He may and will do a great deal for Italy. The Archduke speaks much and affectionately of his dear bride. When we were at luncheon he said to me, "I hope it is a good omen for the future that on this occasion England sits between Austria and Prussia", in which hope I sincerely join.[4]

Even Prince Albert, to whom words of praise did not always come easily, noted within a couple of days of his arrival that Maximilian was 'indeed a very distinguished personage'. To Stockmar he wrote (18 June) that he was 'a remarkable young man, very Anglomane, with nothing of the bigot about him, and liberal in his political views. Charlotte will certainly be happy with him'.[5]

Max was indeed a success in England. The queen's Whig ministers had always regarded continental royalties – particularly the Habsburgs

– with a jaundiced eye, but they were completely taken aback by his tolerant manner, and his somewhat indiscreet readiness to discuss the Italian and Hungarian situations. It was noticed that his views on such subjects were far more liberal than those of the Austrian ambassador. Nonetheless it was strictly a family visit, and Max was anxious not to be drawn into the London social season more than possible. Instead he preferred to accompany the royal family to Handel oratorios at the Crystal Palace or Italian opera at the Haymarket, or visit Charlotte's grandmother, the widowed Queen Marie Amelie of France, or his Orleans cousins at Twickenham.

The impression that Maximilian's family visit had become some kind of unexpectedly successful state visit was viewed with jealousy and apprehension on the continent. In Vienna, Francis Joseph and his ministers were disgruntled when they heard that he was discussing politics with Queen Victoria, and they were angered by an unwise suggestion from Lord John Russell that the ideal solution to the Hungarian problem would be to make Hungary a separate kingdom under King Ferdinand Maximilian. Meanwhile, in Paris, Napoleon was uneasy at these signs of a *rapprochement* between England and Austria, after his recent efforts to cultivate Anglo-French understanding. In Italy Count Camillo di Cavour, prime minister of Piedmont, feared that a liberally-minded, pro-English archduke of Austria would ultimately prove a greater obstacle to the unification of Italy than tyrants of Radetsky's stamp.

A few days after his departure from England, Prince Albert (newly created prince consort) wrote:

> You have conquered my sincerest friendship, which, resting as it does on a similarity in our modes of feeling and thinking, promises to be firmly knit for life by the ties of kinship.[6]

Albert attended the wedding in Brussels cathedral on 27 July. Superficially it was a magnificent ceremony, with a radiant bride and a dashing groom, attired as an Austrian admiral with the Order of the Golden Fleece around his neck, the centre of attention. Already plagued by ill-health, and full of heartache at the thought of seeing his beloved eldest daughter to be married only six months later, Albert was less perceptive than usual. He only saw a favourite niece and an Austrian archduke whom he admired greatly as beginning a long and successful partnership together. Maximilian himself had been a little discomfited by the sight of Charlotte's emotional outbursts at leaving father and home, and he would be again three days after the wedding ceremony when he had to carry her, exhausted from sobbing and on the point of fainting, from her mother's grave at Laeken. Yet neither was as perceptive as the prince of Saxe-Weimar, who commented that while the young princess had an elegant disposition and an excellent figure, 'she has a rather strange look and is totally lacking in charm and grace'. Maximilian had been at the centre of an apparently triumphant point of contact with the English court. He was to pay dearly for this success.

Jealousy of Maximilian had not been the only cloud on the horizon in Vienna. On his return with Charlotte, he was soon acquainted with the unhappy situation at home. The empress had developed from a shy and wayward girl into a spoiled, obstinate young woman who took a malicious delight in refusing to carry out her obligations. Her elder daughter Sophie had died at the age of twenty-one months, and Elizabeth had temporarily shut herself and her fits of weeping away from the world. As yet she had conspicuously failed to produce an heir to the throne, for her only surviving child was a daughter, Gisela. The emperor was finding her progressively more difficult to manage, while the Archduchess Sophie despaired of ever getting her to perform her expected duties. It was no wonder that she looked approvingly on Charlotte, who was not only pretty but well-educated and seemed healthy enough. Maximilian was still his brother's heir, and it might be his children who would reign one day over the Austrian empire.

In view of what was to happen within the next ten years, it was ironic that the archduchess compared her second daughter-in-law so favourably with the empress.

After the visit of Maximilian and Charlotte to Vienna and its attendant festivities, Elizabeth returned tearfully to her rooms. Francis Joseph was about to resume his tour of Hungary which had been interrupted by their daughter's death and his brother's arrival, but Elizabeth was in no state to accompany him. She refused to eat properly, withdrew into herself so completely that nobody was allowed to accompany her on her long walks and rides, and even talked of suicide. At length the emperor, worried beyond endurance, recommended that her mother and sisters should come and visit her in the hope that they might cheer her up.

Though the doctors felt that she should not bear another child in her nervous overwrought state, by Christmas 1857 she was expecting again. This time she was desperate to present her husband and his empire with a son, knowing how acute disappointment had been when two archduchesses had appeared. On 21 August 1858, after a particularly difficult labour in which – according to a midwife – she had nightmare visions of the fall of the Habsburg dynasty and red flags in the streets of Vienna, she gave birth to a son, Rudolf.

Queen Victoria and the prince consort were in Germany at the time, visiting Prince and Princess Frederick William of Prussia at Babelsberg. The queen wrote to the emperor (22 August):

> I beg Your Imperial Majesty to accept my expression of most sincere thanks for the kindness you showed in sending Baron Koller to bring

congratulations on the occasion of my arrival in Germany, and for the letter which you wrote in such kind and affectionate terms. Today it is the turn of the prince and myself to offer our congratulations on the occasion of the successful accouchement of the Empress and the birth of a son, an event of the greatest importance for you and your Empire, which makes us truly rejoice.

We send our wishes for the well-being of the Empress and of the newborn child. Your Majesty is very kind to wish to be associated with the great happiness which we feel in being reunited with our beloved daughter, and in having the satisfaction of seeing her happy in her new country.[7]

The emperor duly replied (28 August):

I have been truly touched by the congratulations which Your Majesty has conveyed to me with such cordiality on the happy occasion of my son's birth. The domestic happiness which you yourself enjoy to such a high degree will give you the measure of the joy which the Empress and I feel. We sincerely thank Your Majesty for the most affectionate terms in which you have conveyed Your Majesty's and the Prince's kind wishes.

From the bottom of my heart I hope Your Majesty and I will soon have occasion to meet personally. At such a time it is important that we maintain mutually intimate relations and that these individual wishes of mine are identical with the political interests of our countries.[8]

Behind such formal messages of congratulation and thanks lay an interesting coincidence and a gentle awareness of an uncertain continental situation.

The coincidence was that, only five months after the birth of Crown Prince Rudolf, Princess Frederick William of Prussia, enjoying a visit that August from her parents in her new and far from happy German home, would bring into the world a future crown prince and emperor, her first child William. Both Rudolf and William would suffer from handicaps from the cradle onwards, the former from excessive Habsburg interbreeding and a morbid fear of insanity, the latter from a severely dislocated left arm which never recovered from its natal injury. There the coincidences ended, for the two princes who might have reigned and ruled as emperors side by side had fate played her part, grew up totally out of sympathy with each other. The eventual accession of one was to prove a decisive factor in the tragic destiny of the other.

The uncertainty was related to Napoleon's devious behaviour. Prince Albert's fears about the increase in the size of the French navy and new fortifications on the French coast had not been allayed by a visit from Queen Victoria and himself to Cherbourg in August 1858, immediately before their journey to Germany. The emperor of the French was crafty enough to let his distinguished guests see the ramparts and vessels, thereby giving the impression that he would hardly have done so if he intended to use them against England. Yet the charm which had worked so well on Queen Victoria three years earlier was conspicuous by its absence. Still smarting from the knowledge that an assassination attempt on him and the Empress Eugenie in January had been perpetrated by Italian conspirators in England and aided by bombs from Birmingham, he asked sarcastically if England still expected an invasion, and complained of attacks on himself in the British press.

In London, Windsor, and Vienna, royal and ministerial minds were much preoccupied over Napoleonic ambitions. A meeting between the emperor of the French and Count Cavour in June, and his declaration that he would support Piedmont in war against Austria, provided it was undertaken for a non-revolutionary cause, alarmed many. It was widely known that he wanted Savoy and Nice to be ceded to France, and in the event of Italian victory these would be his prize. He assumed that England, Russia and Prussia would remain neutral. Russia, everyone knew, had promised to leave Napoleon to his own devices in Italy as a means of revenge after Austrian neutrality in the Crimean war. Prussia, meanwhile, fancied herself as leader of the German confederation. England still sympathised with the cause of Italian unity.

But an over-confident Napoleon took English opinion and support too far for granted. By the end of 1858, it had become necessary to inform him that any attempt by France to embark on a war of Italian liberation against Austria would find no sympathy on the other side of the English channel. Queen Victoria wrote (9 December) to her foreign secretary Lord Malmesbury:

> The Queen is much alarmed at what Lord Cowley writes as to the Emperor Napoleon's supposed intentions to bring on a war in Italy. Whatever can be done to turn the Emperor's mind from such a project ought to be done. If he makes war in Italy it must in all probability lead to war with Germany, and, if with Germany, will embrace Belgium, and if so must, according to our guarantees, draw us into the quarrel, and France may thus have the whole of Europe against her, as in 1814 and 1815.[9]

The following day, Malmesbury assured her that the emperor had officially denied such reports, and that no warlike preparations were being made in France. Little did he know that a secret arrangement with King Victor Emmanuel of Sardinia, by which the combined armies of both monarchs would drive the Austrians out of Italy, was being made; a confederation of Italy would thus be created; Savoy and Nice would be ceded to France, and the king's daughter of sixteen would marry Napoleon's dissolute thirty-six-year-old cousin Napoleon Jerome ('Plon-Plon').

Only a month earlier, the possibility of another visit from Queen Victoria to her daughter in Germany had been discussed. This prompted a strangely veiled letter from Francis Joseph (14 November):

> The brevity of the sojourn which Your Majesty proposes to make on the continent and which you intend to devote exclusively to your family, deprives me, to my great regret, of the good fortune of making your personal acquaintance on this occasion.
>
> As Your Majesty will find yourself near the frontiers of my Empire, I wish at least to offer you my congratulations in writing and to express how much I sympathise with the tender emotions which you must feel at this moment in seeing your cherished daughter again, surrounded as she is by affection in her new country. . .[10]

These pleasantries regarding the approaching confinement which would make Queen Victoria a grandmother masked what must have been an unconscious desire to seek in more positive terms the hand of British friendship.

Family considerations, as so often, played their part in complicating an issue on which the peace of Europe might have depended. Queen Victoria and the prince consort – particularly the latter – were forlornly building their hopes on an united liberal Germany under Prussian leadership, a plan which they had attempted to put into effect with the marriage of Vicky and Fritz. They were moreover distracted by Vicky's pregnancy and alarming ill-health, resulting in an extremely difficult labour (far worse than that of the Empress Elizabeth in August) in January 1859 during which both mother and baby son almost died. At the court of Windsor, therefore, Prussia was paramount. Even though Bismarck, still a diplomat whose political ambitions were not yet realised, was waiting in the wings, Austro-Prussian rivalry was already discernible. Victoria and Albert could hardly be expected to offer Austria open support, in spite of the queen's expression of views to King Leopold that feeling in Britain against the Emperor Napoleon was intense:

> I think yet that if Austria is strong and well prepared and Germany strong and well inclined towards us (as Prussia certainly is) France

will not be so eager to attempt what I firmly believe would end in
the Emperor's downfall.[11]

Here was, or what might have been, a heaven-sent opportunity for
Francis Joseph and Victoria to renew greater contact, perhaps even
meet, and at least give a demonstration of solidarity to pave the way
for firmer Anglo-Austrian understanding – or to warn Napoleon off.

It is easy to be wise after the event, but the reasons which might
have held Francis Joseph back are endless. Was he too proud, too
unimaginative, or too jealous to try and use the friendship built up by
Maximilian in England to valuable political effect? Was he too
distracted by the long-awaited birth of his son and heir, and continued
bickering between his wife and mother? Outside the family, was he
prevented by his ministers, who could not forgive English support in
general and Palmerston's behaviour in particular on behalf of Italian
and Hungarian patriotism?

On such apparently trifling matters rested significant turning points
in nineteenth-century Europe.

Throughout the early months of 1859, diplomacy continued at a
feverish pace. Lord Cowley, British ambassador in Paris, and Malmesbury, tried their utmost to repair damage to Franco-Austrian
relations, Cowley by mediating with Napoleon and Malmesbury by
addressing the Austrian chief minister Count Buol, an arrogant and
inept statesman once described as like 'a locomotive which does not
know where it is going and, when asked, answers only with steam
and whistling'.[12]

In March, Tsar Alexander II proposed a European congress to
which all countries should send representatives. Under the malign
influence of Buol, Francis Joseph demanded disarmament from Piedmont before he would participate. According to Buol, Piedmont had
taken up a position of 'permanent aggression' against Austria. By the
end of April he had despatched an ultimatum to Cavour – disarmament within three days or war.

The long-threatened war was swift and inglorious. On 4 June the
Austrian army, commanded by Count Gyulai, superior in both
numbers and equipment, met and attacked the French near the town
of Magenta. After an indecisive battle, Austrian forces retreated and
conceded victory to their foes. Gyulai was relieved of his command,
ostensibly for 'health reasons' and Francis Joseph hurried to the front
in order to try and instill new courage into his men. The important
conflict took place on 24 June where, for the last time, three European
monarchs – the emperors of Austria and the French, and the king of
Sardinia – faced each other at the head of their armies in battle, on a
plain near Solferino. Galvanised into action by news that a Prussian

army was on its way to aid Austria after weeks of indecision, the French and Italians redoubled their efforts. After several hours of fighting in the sweltering midsummer heat, a violent thunderstorm burst overhead as the Austrian forces decided to retreat. Within days it was ascertained that they had suffered over 20,000 casualties, the Franco-Italian forces perhaps as many as 17,000.

Both emperors were so shattered by the sight of this wholesale carnage and slaughter in the supposedly glorious name of war that they embraced each other with ill-concealed relief, and concluded an armistice at Villafranca in July. Lombardy was to be ceded to Napoleon, who would in turn cede it to Piedmont; Austria would retain Venetia; and the other Italian states would form a federation.

The cost of this war had to be measured in more than human casualties on the battlefields, which so shocked the young Swiss tourist Henri Dunant that he was inspired to found the International Red Cross association. In terms of family and inter-family tensions it also left its mark.

Suffering perpetually from overwork and ill-health, the prince consort contemptuously berated 'the boasting of the Austrians and the miserable impotence of their enormous army (which) has brought contempt'[13] on their country. His son-in-law Prince Frederick William, furious that Germany's ally had been defeated long before Prussian forces had even seen a shot fired, was bitterly rebuked for his 'playing at soldiers'. For the young emperor of Austria, Prince Albert had little sympathy;

> One cannot expect much from a man brought up by Jesuits, by people who recognise only what is bad in their fellow-creatures, always presuppose the uncleanest motives, and hold human nature incapable of noble feelings and thoughts.[14]

In Austria, Francis Joseph's personal reputation had plummeted. Crowds in Vienna were heard to shout 'Abdicate!' when he appeared at a military review, and Maximilian was openly if briefly canvassed as a more suitable emperor of Austria than the failed autocrat. His jealousy resurfaced when Napoleon proposed at Villafranca making Venice an independent state under the archduke's rule, only to be told bluntly that Austria would continue the war rather than see this happen. At the peace conference, signed in Zurich in November, King Leopold tried to argue for Maximilian to have the governorship of Venice. He was told in no uncertain terms that the administration of Austrian provinces was strictly a matter of internal policy. Bitterly Maximilian wrote to Leopold of his depression at seeing the great and once-powerful monarchy slowly sinking into decline 'through incompetence and muddle-headedness for which there is neither excuse nor explanation'.[15] His resentment was made more acute by his brother's chivalrous but vain attempts to save the thrones of their dispossessed cousins in the former kingdoms of Tuscany and Modena.

Austria was in a state of acute crisis, her future threatened by bankruptcy and fear of revolution. Two much-respected statesmen, Count Szechenyi and the minister of finance Baron Bruck, committed suicide, one after persecution by the Habsburg police, the other after being wrongfully indicted in a case of embezzlement of army funds. Several generals and ministers, notably the hated Buol, were either dismissed or demoted. For a while Francis Joseph morosely avoided public appearances as far as possible, uncharacteristically lying low at the Laxenburg palace to brood on his problems.

At home the atmosphere between his mother and wife had deteriorated even further. Elizabeth had become thinner and more nervous still, deeply sensitive to the slightest word of criticism, and seeing enemies everywhere. Sophie appreciated, in a way that her daughter-in-law neither would nor could, that the last thing the emperor wanted at this low point in his fortunes was a new round of family rows.

The main cause of friction was the upbringing of Rudolf. His attendants were driven to distraction by contradictory orders from both women. Elizabeth was a possessive mother but in her nervous state temperamentally unsuited to look after the sickly infant on her own. Despite her domineering nature, the experienced archduchess knew far better what was good for her grandson, and was genuinely upset that the empress was behaving so unreasonably.

During the closing months of 1859 Elizabeth gave every impression of being still very much in love with her husband, recognising how desperately he needed comfort, notwithstanding her emotional immaturity. At times of crisis she was capable of drawing on inner reserves of strength, as her visits to soldiers in hospitals proved. Yet, as was only to be expected, there were conspicuous faults on both sides. She was incapable of making a sustained effort; spontaneous affection and generosity one day could be replaced by paranoia and tantrums the next. She was also too proud to admit that her mother-in-law might be right, that hectoring advice Sophie gave about her duties as a mother, wife and above all empress, was kindly meant if perhaps tactlessly given.

Francis Joseph's greatest fault as a family man was that he had no imagination. The qualities of dedication to duty which served him well as emperor were not those required for a successful husband. In his way he loved her deeply, as his anxious letters from the front in Italy showed. But he could not understand his wife's complex, over-sensitive character, or realise that there was anything of value in her ideas, that she had a vivid and active mind sorely needing an useful outlet.

On their visit to Hungary in 1857 Elizabeth had been fascinated by the country and people. In the vitality of Magyar life, music and horses, she found a kindred spirit. The Hungarians were quick to see that they had a genuine friend at court. Later, when she begged Francis Joseph to make some concessions to the Magyar constitution and national aspirations, the most he would concede was that 'there are some good points in what you say'. Privately he was too ready to agree with his mother that the only reason Elizabeth was interested in the Hungarians was because they appealed to her sense of the picturesque.

During 1860 a sequence of diplomatic events and activities, personal and political, coincided with the supreme crisis of Francis Joseph's married life.

Elizabeth's sister Marie had married Prince Francis of Naples. A few months after his accession to the Neapolitan throne, Garibaldi and his thousand volunteers descended upon Sicily, invaded Naples, and king and queen were forced to flee. Queen Maria Sophia, as she had become, entreated her sister to use what influence she could with her husband to save their throne. Plagued by internal difficulties with his government, it was with a heavy heart that the emperor had to decline his help. After Austria's crushing defeat in Italy the previous year, he could not embroil himself again there, and all he could do was to offer his dispossessed relations a safe haven and sympathy.

Meanwhile, in July Francis Joseph was due to meet the prince regent of Prussia at Toplitz. It was a private conference in which the prince consort took a keen interest, relating – as he had expected – to the future of Germany, more open and more punctual support for Austria from Prussia in future lest France should continue to aid Italian revolutionaries at Austrian expense. In a memorandum to Lord John Russell (4 August), based on a letter from the prince regent, Prince Albert described Francis Joseph as 'self-possessed and open, speaking of Russia and England without any bitterness'.[16]

Even at this stage, though, royalty and ministers alike throughout Europe looked with suspicion on Albert's preoccupation, or ill-disguised meddling as they might have it, with foreign affairs. Under normal circumstances, the way might otherwise have been paved for him or Queen Victoria, or both, to meet Francis Joseph for at least an informal discussion from which a greater measure of personal understanding might result.

In September the queen and Albert travelled to Germany for a family reunion at Coburg. That the idea of further meetings was envisaged is clear from an exchange of letters with Palmerston, once again prime minister but since the Crimean war on much better terms with his sovereign and her husband and Russell. Palmerston advised Her Majesty (20 September) that

a meeting at present between Your Majesty and the Emperor of Austria, though in many respects likely to be useful, would on

the whole be so liable to misconstruction, and would prove such a
fertile source of misrepresentation, that it would be better to avoid
it. Such a meeting would undoubtedly be useful to the Emperor of
Austria, by reason of the good advice which he would receive from
Your Majesty, and from His Royal Highness the Prince Consort;
but Your Majesty will probably be able to find some other way of
conveying to the Emperor counsel calculated to save him from
some of the dangers by which he appears to be beset.[17]

The queen replied to Russell (21 September) that

> while such an interview might for many reasons have been
> desirable, under present circumstances it might lead to much talk
> and to many rumours which might do harm, or at any rate give rise
> to useless conjectures. It would therefore be better to "nip this
> project in the bud" as Lord John suggests, but care should be taken
> to do this in such a manner as not to let it appear that there was any
> disinclination on the Queen's part to meet the Emperor of
> Austria.[18]

What Francis Joseph's feelings at the prospect of such a meeting were
will never be known, but he had to content himself with a brief message
(24 September):

> The sojourn of Your Majesty on the continent gives me the
> occasion to express with my sincere congratulations the lively
> interest that I take in everything which concerns your happiness.
>   I have charged Lieutenant-General Count Mensdorff, whom
> Your Majesty has deigned to honour with your kindness and who
> enjoys my complete confidence as the interpreter to you of these
> feelings.
>   I assure Your Majesty of the high value which I attach to the
> friendship which binds us and which, I hope, will only become
> closer in the presence of the growing dangers in the political
> situation. . .[19]

In view of a rather indiscreet though not untrue comment to King
Leopold earlier that month, it may have been just as well that the
sovereigns did not meet. When Garibaldi invaded Naples, Queen
Maria Sophia was said to have told her vacillating husband that if he did
not place himself at the head of the troops remaining loyal to them, she
would do so herself. Queen Victoria lamented the distressing state of
affairs in Italy, 'but really the miserable, weak and foolish conduct of
the King of Naples and the squabbles of the whole family takes away all
one's sympathy!'[20]

In October, Francis Joseph met the tsar at Warsaw. Throughout European courts, it was looked forward to with eager anticipation. Ex-King Francis of Naples hoped for armed intervention in Italy to restore his throne. Elsewhere, it was rumoured that Austria and Russia would become reconciled and demand a revision of the 1856 treaty of Paris, in order to guarantee Austria from attack in Venetia or Hungary. But nothing came of it, politically at least. The Russian foreign minister Count Gortschakoff was even less forgiving than his master, and both emperors returned to their respective capitals with nothing to show for their efforts.

Rumours of a more explosive kind reached Viennese society at this time. It was whispered that the emperor had had other reasons for visiting Warsaw – namely, to renew acquaintance with a Polish countess whom he had known before his marriage, and who could fulfil his physical needs in a way the empress could or would not. No reliable evidence exists. It may have been the by-product of scandal-mongering prevalent at every court and society, and which Queen Victoria had had cause to deplore especially in relation to Austria.

This has been advanced as one reason for the complete physical and mental breakdown which the Empress Elizabeth suffered at this time. A more likely explanation (again, for which no convincing documentary evidence is available) has been offered. Her wrists and knees had been disfigured by unsightly swellings at the joints for some time, and court doctors could not diagnose or cure them. Seeking opinion elsewhere, heavily veiled and under an assumed name, she consulted another doctor who did not know or recognise her. He told her that she was suffering from an unpleasant contagious disease. In other words, she was venereally infected.

Discovery of her husband's infidelity, the plight of her sister, inability to take any more from her mother-in-law, suspected tuberculous infection of the throat, or some similar illness – the possible reasons are endless. All that is known for certain was that the emperor returned from Warsaw to find his wife in a state of acute distress. She insisted that she must go as far away as possible. From all corners of the empire, suggestions were made, but she was adamant at going further. Her choice fell on Madeira, which had been described to her by Maximilian as a veritable paradise. Even better, it was sufficiently remote from the likelihood of resident or neighbouring royalties and Austrian officials.

The emperor tried to delay her departure, on the grounds that there was no imperial yacht ready or capable of such a journey in winter. She accordingly applied to Queen Victoria to lend her a vessel. Alarmed at the news from Vienna, the sympathetic queen generously placed her yacht *Victoria and Albert* at her disposal, as 'being the only really fast and comfortable vessel and she goes over tomorrow to carry the beautiful, fragile young Empress alone without husband and children to a distant land! May it not be too late'.[21] With loan of the yacht came an invitation for Elizabeth to visit her in England on the way, but this was the last thing she wanted. Through the British ambassador Lord Bloomfield she declined this on the grounds of ill health and the fact that she was travelling incognito. Within a fortnight, though, Queen Victoria had 'a most affectionate letter from the Empress herself written from the yacht' in which she was apparently delighted with everything 'and hoping to visit me on her way back'[22] – knowing Elizabeth, probably an expression of goodwill which she had no intention of honouring.

Stormy weather accompanied Elizabeth and her retinue to Madeira, but she was unaffected by seasickness and seemed to enjoy the excitement of rough sea. By the time they arrived at the island she was in visibly better health. For four months she surrounded herself with her dogs, ponies and books, and free of tensions of court life she experienced a feeling of contentment she had not known since her marriage. Occasionally she would give way to melancholy and long to see her husband and children again, and she would issue orders to depart at once, only to cancel them moments later. She was relieved to hear that her sister the ex-queen of Naples was safe, and the death of Queen Victoria's mother the duchess of Kent in March 1861 moved her to pen a gracious letter of condolence the following month.

Thanks to one member of the empress's suite, this Anglo-Austrian connection was to have one extremely beneficial result in years to come. This member was Prince Francis of Teck, then aged twenty-three. The son of Duke Alexander of Wurttemberg and a Hungarian beauty Countess Claudia Rhèdey, he was a particular favourite of the emperor, who commissioned him into the imperial army when he came of age. Francis was captivated by the royal yacht, and for him it was the start of a lifelong admiration for all things British. A few years later he was invited to England by a royal family desperate to marry off the jolly, outgoing but distressingly overweight Princess Mary of Cambridge. In 1866 they were married and their first child, also named Mary, was destined to become the wife of Queen Victoria's grandson, later King George V.

Francis Joseph wrote to his wife regularly, entreating her to return. Missing her tenderly, he obtained a detailed map of Madeira, so that he could try and follow her movements on it from descriptions in her letters. By the end of April she was on her way back to Trieste to meet him. On the way the yacht stopped at Malta, where empress and English governor got on very well together. She was grateful at their respect for her wish for privacy, while he was relieved to be spared the trouble of a state visit. In May, with tears in his eyes, Francis Joseph met and embraced his wife off the isle of Lacroma in the Adriatic Sea. After a brief visit to Maximilian and Charlotte, rendered none too happy by mutual jealousy between both women, they returned to Vienna. But after a few weeks back in the capital she fell again into a rapid decline. It was rumoured that she had only six weeks to live. By midsummer she had fled to Corfu, brushing aside warnings from those who claimed that such a notoriously malaria-ridden island was no place for somebody in her state of health. Lord Bloomfield commented derisively that he had never before heard Corfu recommended by doctors as a summer resort for invalids.

Stories of Elizabeth's imminent demise were soon proved to have been greatly exaggerated. Yet another royal death, one of far greater political consequence, was shortly to transform relationships throughout several European courts.

The prince consort was overtired and had gradually, almost imperceptibly, slipped into a state of mental and physical exhaustion from which he would not recover. A carriage accident in Coburg during the family's visit in October 1860 had left him suffering from delayed shock. Only his mentor Baron Stockmar had the perception to realise that if anything serious happened to Albert, he would die. 'I am sure', the prince confided to Queen Victoria some months later, 'if I had a severe illness, I should give up at once, I should not struggle for life.'[23]

At Osborne in August 1861, Albert received Maximilian and Charlotte for a three-day visit. Though happy to see them again, he was under no illusions that he would hear much in the way of good news about the state of affairs between Austria and Hungary. Though no record of the sojourn from Maximilian's hand survives, it is evident that politics took priority in conversation between both men. Queen Victoria described Max as 'most agreeable, and very clever; he has such good sense too, and is wonderfully fair. Albert was amazingly struck by him'.[24]

Writing to Baron Stockmar (6 September), Albert noted that the couple

> were very friendly, and are both people of no common order.
>   He is satisfied that his brother sincerely means not to let the constitutional regime again become a dead letter, and that he sees his own safety in so acting, but he seemed to me himself to undervalue the Hungarian difficulty, as people in Vienna generally appear to do.[25]

Both the prince consort and Maximilian, being of like-minded liberal sympathies, were fully agreed over the question of greater recognition for Hungary and her constitution. One can also have little doubt that the archduke conveyed Albert's views to Elizabeth, and perhaps reinforced her conviction that the emperor was refusing to face Hungarian problems with adequate attention. It was unfortunate that Elizabeth and Albert were destined never to meet, for on Hungary at least they would have had considerable common ground.

Three months after writing to Stockmar, Albert lay seriously ill with typhoid at Windsor Castle. Queen Victoria was impatient of sickness in others, and it was to their second daughter Alice that he looked instinctively for a more sympathetic nurse. When she told him that she had reported to Vicky in Germany that he was very ill, he corrected her; 'You should have told her I was dying'. Shortly before midnight on 14 December, he died at the age of forty-two.

1. Queen Victoria with the Princess Royal and Prince of Wales, 1842, after a portrait by Edwin Landseer

2. Emperor Francis Joseph, c. 1850

3. Queen Victoria and Albert, Prince Consort, 1859

4a. Archduke Maximilian in uniform as Admiral of the Austrian fleet, c. 1858

4b. Empress Elizabeth, c. 1866

5a. Albert Edward, Prince of Wales, 1883

5b. Alexandra, Princess of Wales, 1883

6a. Empress Elizabeth on horseback, c. 1880

6b. Crown Prince Rudolf and Crown Princess Stephanie, 1884

7a.   William I, German Emperor

7b.   The German Crown Prince Frederick William,
later Emperor Frederick III, 1883

8a. Victoria,
German Empress, later
Empress Frederick, 1888

8b. William II,
German Emperor, 1898

CHAPTER 3

'This wretched Mexico'

After the prince consort's death, there was a change in the relationship between the British and Austrian reigning families. Queen Victoria had been content to leave contacts to the exchange of correspondence, though she was destined to meet Francis Joseph four times during her widowhood, and would also see Elizabeth and Rudolf on fleeting occasions. The prince consort himself would undoubtedly have liked to meet the emperor, increasingly concerned as he was towards the end of his short life with the question of German unity, worried by rivalry between Austria and Prussia, and alarmed by the increasing intransigence of King William I, whose reactionary behaviour as monarch proved he was not the liberally-minded gentleman Albert had unhappily deluded himself into thinking he was.

Now that Queen Victoria was 'the widow of Windsor', the British monarchy was represented increasingly at both social and diplomatic levels by Albert Edward, prince of Wales. Because of his easy-going nature and as a result of various personal relationships he made during the remaining thirty-nine years of his mother's reign, Austria loomed prominently in his affections. His visits to the Habsburg empire were mainly for pleasure and rarely concerned with politics. As a social playground, it came second to France in his estimation, and with the advantage over France that it did not become a republic during his lifetime.

The first contact between the prince of Wales and Emperor Francis Joseph took the shape of a letter from the former, written on behalf of Queen Victoria from Osborne House (5 January 1862). Addressed to 'Sir, my *brother and cousin*', it read:

> The Queen my beloved Mother has sustained an overwhelming loss in the death of my most beloved and revered Father, His Royal Highness The Prince Consort, Prince Albert of Saxe-Coburg Gotha, Duke of Saxony, which took place at Windsor Castle at Ten Minutes before Eleven o'Clock on the night of the 14th ultimo, after a short illness, in the 43rd. year of his Age. –

Your *Imperial Majesty* can well conceive the utter desolation and
grief of The Queen under the unexpected bereavement which
Her Majesty, Her Family, and Her Country have undergone.

Under these deeply afflicting circumstances I have been
commanded to write, in this one instance, on behalf of my
disconsolate mother, for the purpose of announcing to *Your
Imperial Majesty* this fatal event. – The Queen is persuaded that
You will kindly receive the notification as from herself, and that
You will give Her Your affectionate sympathy under the heavy
trial with which it has pleased Divine Providence to visit her.

I request Your *Imperial Majesty* to accept these Assurances of
the invariable Friendship and highest Consideration. . .[1]

Personal contact was not long in following. The grieving Queen
Victoria was resolute that her late husband's plans should be carried
out strictly according to the letter. As far as their eldest son and heir
was concerned, this meant his tour in the east under supervision of his
governor, General Bruce, followed by marriage to Princess Alexandra
of Denmark. The prince must observe strict incognito, and he could
visit sovereigns privately, but not accept other invitations.

On 5 February the prince took leave of his mother at Osborne. His
itinerary would take him through Germany and Austria to Trieste,
where he was to embark for Egypt. En route he was offered
hospitality from many quarters, not always with the queen's full
approval, but nonetheless not easy to avoid. After a family visit to
Darmstadt and Prince Louis of Hesse, recently betrothed to his sister
Alice, he reached Vienna on 13 February.

In spite of Queen Victoria's orders to the contrary, Lord Bloomfield
had notified the Austrian court and government of his impending
arrival. It was only with difficulty that the ever-chivalrous emperor
was dissuaded from giving his guest the full round of ceremonial
welcome, such as a traditional guard of honour, a state dinner, and
military parade. The prince stayed privately at a hotel, but the
emperor called regularly and guided him round the main public
buildings. According to the future King Edward VII's first official
biographer, Sir Sidney Lee, 'the Prince always remembered pleasantly
his first experience of the Austrian Emperor's smiling but taciturn
courtliness'.[2]

At Trieste, where the royal yacht *Osborne* had been sent to meet
him, the prince was entertained briefly by Maximilian and Charlotte.
With some trepidation they crossed to Venice, where the name of
Austria was held in great contempt. Lord Russell had to warn the
British agent in Venice that any demonstration by the Venetians in the
prince of Wales' honour might offend Austria, and it was vital for him
to preserve his 'strictest incognito'. Yet it was only a few years before

this most cosmopolitan and widely-travelled of princes would find such precautions unnecessary.

Were Francis Joseph and his advisers secretly hoping to woo Britain, partly through dynastic personal contacts with her ruling house, away from her Prussian allegiance and win a measure of sympathy for Austria in her German confederation struggle? Though the heir to the Prussian throne was married to the queen's eldest daughter, and this counted for much in pro-Prussian feeling at Windsor, it was widely recognised that the British government had little affection for Prussia. Even if Palmerston, Russell and the rest of the British cabinet placed Austria no higher in their estimation, a few tactful Habsburg overtures might still bear fruit, now that the prince consort was dead.

For events, ultimately crucial to the future of both Prussia and Austria, had moved speedily since the beginning of 1862. No longer held in check by the younger Coburg prince whom he had openly affected to despise but really feared to some extent, King William of Prussia fell foul of his *Landtag*, temporarily lost his nerve on the vexed issue of internal constitutional reforms, and threatened to abdicate in favour of Crown Prince Frederick William. When the latter hesitated, William appointed Otto von Bismarck his minister-president. Bismarck, then ambassador at St Petersburg, had a 'reputation for wanton brutality', and was feared throughout Germany, except by the conservative Junker ruling classes in Prussia, for his ruthlessness. In Austria the appointment was particularly unnerving, for Francis Joseph realised that here was the man who personified Prussian ambitions to lead the confederation at his own empire's expense.

In Berlin the crown prince and princess of Prussia distrusted and feared Bismarck. With their openly liberal sympathies, they recognised in him a reactionary of the deepest dye. After a few days of unmitigated rudeness from the king, and in a mood of black despair, they eagerly accepted an offer to join the prince of Wales on part of his Mediterranean cruise. Soon after taking their leave of him at Rome in November, they started on their journey home through the Austrian empire. Throughout Venetia they were ceremoniously received, and in Verona they were welcomed by the Austrian commander in Italy, Ludwig von Benedek. Prince Frederick William was impressed by his 'simple, soldierly manner very much, also his correct military decisions at which he arrives through determination and wide experience'.[3] Ironically, both men would be facing each other on the battlefield only four years later.

They were greeted in Vienna with a large family dinner presided over by Francis Joseph and Elizabeth, who had returned that summer in better spirits after wintering in Venice. In a letter to Queen Victoria (17 December), the crown princess had much to say about her hosts.

The emperor and empress, she commented, were both very kind and amicable to them both, though Elizabeth

> . . .seems very shy and timid and talks very little – indeed it is
> very difficult to keep up a conversation with her as she seems to
> know very little and to take interest in but very few things. . .She
> spoke of you and darling Papa and is very fond of everything
> English. It is quite a pleasure to sit and look at her she is so
> handsome. The Emperor seems to dote on her, but I did not
> observe that she did on him. He is most insignificant, very plain
> to begin with (which you would not suppose from his pictures
> and photographs), he looked so old and wrinkled and his reddish
> moustache and whiskers are very unbecoming, he had little or no
> conversation and is altogether exceedingly *unbedeutend* (insignifi-
> cant), such a contrast to Max. The Emperor is very kind to Fritz
> and calls him Du and leads him about everywhere. . .[4]

From a personal angle, the visit was successful enough, but politically nothing was accomplished. At one point Fritz told the emperor that Prussia wished the imperial cabinet to bring some influence to bear on the German central states to moderate their hostility, but Francis Joseph did not reply. Secretly he longed to ask that Berlin should rather drop her anti-Austrian attitude.

Francis Joseph's forebodings were soon proved correct. In the summer of 1863 he attempted to summon a conference at Frankfurt, inviting all German sovereigns to discuss the constitution and future of the confederation. Though not exactly a liberal monarch himself, he had long since seen the virtue of tempering traditional Habsburg autocracy. After Solferino he had begun to realise, after a fashion, that the destiny of the component parts of his empire could no longer be controlled by absolute monarchy, especially if the absolute monarch himself had paid the ultimate penalty in war with another nation of being defeated in battle. He had revived provincial diets in Hungary and Bohemia, and in Austria he decreed a constitution and granted further powers to parliament – 'we are going to have a little parliamentarianism, but all power stays in my hands'.[5] Now, with commendable foresight, he wanted to provide the initiative for 'the last chance for the various princes to save themselves before they are swept away by the growing tide of revolution'.[6]

King William of Prussia wished to attend, but Bismarck would not countenance this. (Only the previous year he had secretly told Disraeli, a future British prime minister, that he intended 'at the earliest opportunity to make war on Austria'). He pleaded, cajoled, raged at his master, and eventually won his case by declaring that the

invitation to Prussia had arrived so late that it was an insult.
Francis Joseph nonetheless tried his hardest, and the conference
opened on 17 August. As in the Crimean war, he soon discovered that
it was quite impossible to please everybody at once. On this occasion,
if the conference had been cancelled, he would have been accused of
unwillingness to make an effort in the interests of continental harmony. Instead the talks opened, and both King William and the crown
prince felt that the honour of Prussia and the Hohenzollerns had been
insulted. Proceedings should not, they maintained, have opened
without Prussian representation.

By coincidence, Queen Victoria was about to visit Coburg, to see
the widow of Baron Stockmar. Despite the crown prince's half-
hearted desire to forget the whole affair, both he and the princess went
to talk to her. In the course of conversation, he was persuaded that it
was only right his father should swallow his pride and cooperate with
Austria. From all accounts except Bismarck's, he believed that the
Emperor Francis Joseph gave the impression of being a gentleman and
not a hypocrite, and in any case the peace of Europe should not be
jeopardised by petty feelings of personal vanity.

Queen Victoria offered to try and use her powers of persuasion to
get King William to go to Frankfurt. Nobody was convinced that she
would succeed, for it was her first journey abroad as a widow and she
was guided less by her experience – or lack of it – as a diplomat than
by a mission to do what her husband would have expected of her; but
she promised to make the effort. When King William paid her a
courtesy call at the end of August, she stressed how much she
favoured a rapprochement between Prussia and Austria. Concealing
his impatience with the ghost of the prince consort, and primed
carefully by Bismarck, the king told her that ministers in Vienna were
deliberately planning to ruin Prussia. He added that Francis Joseph
was bent on increasing the influence of the Catholic church, and as the
two leading Protestant powers in Europe, Britain and Prussia should
combine to keep Austria in check. Realising that it was his minister-
president speaking and not the king himself, Queen Victoria sadly
broke off the discussion.

Without King William, the conference achieved nothing. In
summing up, Francis Joseph could only voice his hopes that their
efforts might be crowned by another reunion at the earliest possible
date, and that next time all members of the confederation would be
represented. But gloomily in private he echoed Duke Ernest of Saxe
Coburg's verdict that it would be the last time German princes would
meet as friends and not at daggers drawn.

Queen Victoria cordially invited the emperor to meet her at Schloss
Rosenau. As they had had to forgo similar social calls on her visits to
Germany in 1858 and 1860, he could hardly refuse, but he made it

clear that this was merely to be '*la visite de politesse*'. This first meeting of queen and emperor, on 3 September, lasted about three hours. Only the duke of Coburg was present with them. Describing the emperor as 'very quiet, simple and unaffected, not talkative, but very dignified', she reported to her daughter (5 September) that though she had little opportunity for conversation,

> . . .I took care to say what you wished, and repeatedly to observe upon the necessity of Prussia's being put upon a footing of equality. He assured me that this was his wish, and that there was no other wish in Germany – that I might assure you (I asked what I should say) of the very friendly disposition of Austria. He said (and did Uncle Ernest) that the plan would be submitted to the King and if he would not accept it, they hoped he would state his objections which would then be considered. He regretted the King's non-appearance and lays the whole blame at the door of Bismarck and not of the King.[7]

In reply, the crown princess wrote (8 September) that her father-in-law the king was anxious for an understanding between both, but Austria had 'really not behaved well towards us – the feeling of resentment here is as general with all parties as it is strong'.[8]

While Francis Joseph was beset with problems pertaining to the German confederation, Maximilian was likewise pondering his position. After the Austrians were driven out of Italy in 1859, Max and Charlotte resigned themselves to a life of leisure in their fairytale palace Miramare, on the Adriatic coast near Trieste. Though he seemed prepared to bide his time, gloomily accepting that his brother would probably never offer him employment again, his ambitious wife longed for responsibility and power. As such, both of them were ideal candidates for any vacant throne which might be offered them in the unstable world of nineteenth-century European diplomacy.

Napoleon was keen to restore good relations with Austria after the Italian war. In the autumn of 1861, he held out to Maximilian the prospect of the most prestigious gift he could offer – that of the imperial throne of Mexico.

Mexico had been a Spanish colony until 1821. A constitutional monarchy founded in that year was overthrown in 1824 and the country became a republic, torn by civil war which resulted in the arrival of French troops brought in on the pretext of unpaid debts. By 1861, they had apparently succeeded in routing troops under General Juarez, and Napoleon intended to establish an empire under French patronage, with the continuing presence of his army as a guarantee of security.

Napoleon knew how to play on human vanity to his advantage, and Maximilian was attracted by the idea of independence from his brother, moreover one which involved reigning over an empire potentially richer and greater than Austria. Charlotte was likewise thrilled at the vision of becoming an empress. In Vienna, feelings were very different. The Archduchess Sophie was firmly opposed to such a hazardous venture; at the same time, with Crown Prince Rudolf being frequently ill and perhaps not destined to attain his majority, she recognised that Maximilian and Charlotte might still succeed Francis Joseph on the Austrian throne. The emperor himself was unimpressed by the spectre of an Austrian archduke wearing a Mexican crown. Having once branded Napoleon as 'that arch-rogue', and bearing in mind his reputation as the sober realist, the ever-cautious one, it was strange that he did not reject the offer outright on Maximilian's behalf as being beneath the Habsburgs' dignity. But the chance of ridding himself of this tiresome and too-popular brother who thirsted for power was tempting. He let it be known that acceptance of the Mexican crown was out of the question unless offered by the Mexican people themselves and guaranteed by the maritime powers.

Meanwhile an existing throne closer to home had recently been vacated. In October 1862 the Greeks deposed their unpopular and childless Wittelsbach monarch King Otto. Not wishing to do away with the monarchical form of government, they chose Queen Victoria's second son Prince Alfred, who received 95% of votes cast in a plebiscite. Unfortunately for them, but fortunately for Alfred, he was ineligible under the terms of a London protocol signed in 1830. Palmerston and Russell thought Maximilian 'far too good for Mexico', and nominated him as a possible king of Greece, hoping to spare him from an uncertain fate as Napoleon's pawn.

But Maximilian and Francis Joseph were united in thinking it the height of bad taste for the British government to offer him the crown of a country from which their cousin had had to flee on an English man-o'war. King Leopold, who had himself been offered the Hellenic throne in 1830, urged his son-in-law to accept a throne 'of incomparably greater importance than that of Mexico', but could not deflect him from his purpose. He would not consider a crown which had been hawked around unsuccessfully to several other princes,* but asked Leopold if he could secure Palmerston's support for the Mexican candidature, for there lay 'a brilliant future'. Mexico, he maintained, was a country of immense natural riches, while Greece was 'poor in men and money'.

---

* It was eventually accepted by Prince William of Denmark, younger brother of the princess of Wales, who reigned as King George I of Greece.

Negotiations proceeded slowly for a couple of years, while Maximilian (frequently accompanied by Charlotte) conferred with Mexican delegations and the French, studying the situation carefully from every possible aspect.

Reluctantly, King Leopold gave his consent. In September 1863, while Maximilian was still prevaricating, he wrote cautiously to Queen Victoria:

> The undertaking is a perilous one, but if it succeeds it will be one of the greatest and most useful of our time. (Max) has a great wish to distinguish himself, and to get out of his present *dolce far niente*. Charlotte dear is not opposed to it; she is very venturesome and would go with Max to the end of the world; she will be of the greatest use to him; and, if success there is to be, much will be owing to her.[9]

The difference in attitudes between Paris and London was acute. Early in 1864, by which time Maximilian had at last accepted and negotiations were almost complete, Napoleon and Eugenie could not be more fulsome in their affection for Maximilian and Charlotte. If they ever had any twinges of conscience, these were appeased by deceptive reports from Mexico of French victories, both diplomatic and military, in the civil war.

But in London, Queen Victoria welcomed them as fondly as ever – only, however, as members of the family, not as the future emperor and empress of Mexico. She and her ministry made it clear that they could do nothing for the young couple beyond wishing them well, and they did not disguise their convictions that it was a foolhardy enterprise.

At Claremont, there was outspoken criticism. Charlotte's widowed grandmother, Queen Marie Amelie, tried to dissuade her and her husband from accepting. To her and to the exiled Orleans princes, it was quite incomprehensible that a Habsburg could agree to take part in such a scheme hatched by the Bonapartes. Yet glowing French praises, the promise of independence from Vienna, and a new crown, had hardened their joint resolve. As they embraced for the last time, the dowager queen burst into tears, telling Maximilian that it would surely end in his assassination. Charlotte remained stony-faced, but he broke down and wept.

On their final return to Vienna, an unpleasant surprise awaited Maximilian. Already unnerved by sad looks on his parents' faces and entreaties to reconsider his decision from his other elder relations, among them ex-Emperor Ferdinand, he was presented with an act of renunciation which Francis Joseph wished him to sign. This made his consent to Maximilian accepting the crown of Mexico strictly subject to his renouncing for himself and his issue all rights of succession and inheritance in Austria. A furious and humiliated Maximilian asked his mother to intervene. She begged the emperor not to take away his brother's birthright, but Francis Joseph remained obdurate. Only the desperate entreaties of Charlotte and Napoleon prevented Maximilian from renouncing his Mexican ambitions altogether.

After much further negotiation and argument, the most Maximilian could wring from his brother was a guarantee that, if he should be deprived of the throne in Mexico and had to return to Austria, the emperor would take all necessary measures to safeguard his position and presence in the Austrian empire as far as was compatible in the national interest.

At Miramare on 9 April 1864, both brothers signed the 'family pact'. All imperial dignitaries present noticed the reddened eyes and trembling hands of emperor and archduke. As they embraced each other that afternoon, witnesses looked away, for tears streamed down the brothers' faces, as if conscious that they would never see each other again. Only Charlotte was as outwardly impassive as ever.

By coincidence, that same day Queen Victoria confided her views to Crown Princess Frederick William on the subject. Max and Charlotte, she said, had had much annoyance about 'this wretched Mexico which I so fear will end badly for them. It really grieves me deeply'.[10]

Next day, a deputation of Mexicans presented themselves at Miramare and formally offered the crown to Maximilian and Carlota – her new Mexican name. That week, they sailed for their new destiny. Their fate was sealed.

The Mexican empire had been an unwelcome distraction for Francis Joseph from the ever-present shadow cast by Bismarck. In 1864 Prussia and Austria went to war against Denmark over the duchies of Schleswig and Holstein, which King Christian IX of Denmark claimed on his accession to the throne in November 1865. Most of the German states championed the duke of Augustenburg as the duchies' rightful ruler, but in Berlin and Vienna a view prevailed that they should belong to Germany. The Danes were defeated in a swift conflict, and by the convention of Gastein in August 1865, it was agreed that Schleswig should be administered by Prussia, and Holstein by Austria. Suspicion that this was a temporary measure, and part of Bismarck's devious long-term strategy, was soon to be proved.

Already the victors were quarrelling over their spoils of war. Rumours were rife that Prussia, or rather Bismarck, was quite ready to go to war if Austria did not comply with her wishes. Even those who disliked Bismarck were inclined to the national Prussian view. 'You know I am not wildly enthusiastic about Austria,'[11] wrote the crown princess, no admirer of the minister-president, to Queen Victoria in July 1865, a month before the Gastein convention.

By March 1866, it was clear that Bismarck's boasts about war with Austria were no idle threat. Francis Joseph, like the Prussian crown prince, was unhappy about the partitioning of Schleswig and Holstein, and at length he suggested that they should be handed over to the duke of Augustenburg. The diet at Frankfurt representatives endorsed the Augustenburg claim, thereby overruling decisions reached at Gastein.

King William was alarmed by the war fever which had gripped Bismarck and most of his ministers in Berlin. On 16 March he asked the crown prince to write to Queen Victoria, saying he was anxious to accept an offer of mediation if England and her government would arbitrate between Austria and Prussia. 'You again, dearest Mama,' wrote the crown princess, 'may be the means of averting a European conflagration, and it now rests in your dear hands.'[12]

This was not the intention of Bismarck. He told the British ambassador in Berlin coldly that his ministers should address themselves to Vienna, as Austria was the party which threatened to disturb peace. After consulting Lord Russell, Queen Victoria replied sadly to her son-in-law (28 March) that 'the course pursued by the Prussian Government, under the influence of Count Bismarck, makes it very difficult, if not impossible, for England to interfere with her good offices'.[13] By the end of May the queen declared she could do no more. Her foreign minister Lord Clarendon, knowing that Bismarck wielded more power than his sovereign, insisted that the British government was powerless to influence events any further. A pacifist majority in the Prussian *Landtag* suggested an European conference, but Queen Victoria declared that neither she nor her ministers would be a party to any proceedings which would allow Prussia to annex the duchies.

On 15 June 1866 Prussian troops crossed the frontiers of Hanover, Saxony and Hesse. Several small battles forced the Austrians and their allies from the German confederation into retreat, and on 4 July both armies faced each other on a plain near Königgrätz. By nightfall, over 40,000 Austrians had been killed, wounded or taken prisoner, and the rest of their forces were in retreat.

Prussia threatened to advance further into the Austrian empire. King William, a competent soldier but no statesman, would have ordered his troops to invade Vienna instantly if the decision had been left to him. It took an unlikely alliance of Crown Prince Frederick William, who had not wanted war in the first place, and Bismarck, well aware of the necessity of expelling Austria from the German confederation but not antagonising her unduly by depriving her of territory or submitting her to the indignity of occupation, to restrain him.

Peace was signed at Prague in August. Francis Joseph ceded Venetia to Italy; most of Schleswig, Holstein, Hanover, Hesse-Cassel, Nassau and the city of Frankfurt, were absorbed into Prussia. Had it not been for the Salic Law which excluded a princess from inheriting the Hanoverian throne, King William IV of Great Britain and Hanover would not have been succeeded in the latter territory by the late King Ernest Augustus, but instead by their niece Queen Victoria. Ironically, no dissenting British voices were raised in Britain at Prussia's rape of the ancestral home.

Crown Princess Frederick William's acid comments in the aftermath of this short war (11 September) had a curious echo of those made by her father in 1859. It was true, she said, that King William did not wish for war; he was driven to it by 'his clique of bad advisers':

> The Emperor of Austria is blessed with a counterpart of this clique who push him and have pushed him to incur so many dangers and into so many disasters. But as the Austrian state is corrupt, and ours, in spite of bad government, benighted sovereigns and mischievous ministers, is not – it gained the victory; that is the explanation of the whole thing. The Austrians have long been going downhill, but have with a wonderful talent and subtlety succeeded in blinding the world at large and particularly the small German states to this fact; in the eyes of the governments of the small states, Austria kept its own prestige and has plunged its allies into all its own straits.[14]

Thus ran one point of view. A totally different one came from her brother, the prince of Wales, distressed at the 'pain and anxiety' brought about by 'this dreadful war':

> The Prussians, of course, conducted their campaign well, but what a pretty reputation they have left everywhere behind them, plundering and destroying at every turn! . . . I don't doubt it will be a shameful peace that the Prussians will enforce.[15]

As for Emperor Francis Joseph himself, Queen Victoria noted in her journal (7 December) that according to Lord Bloomfield, he 'had grown ten years older, and was terribly cast down'.[16]

Prussian victory over Austria precipitated a move which the Empress Elizabeth had long urged, and of which the prince consort would surely have approved – rapprochement with Hungary. On the recommendation of Baron Ferdinand Beust, prime minister of Saxony who had already won respect for his conciliatory powers between the defeated and victorious states in Germany, work on a new constitution began almost at once. It led to an official compromise, or *Ausgleich*, in which the Austrian empire (with Hungary as a subservient state) became the dual monarchy of Austria-Hungary, and Francis Joseph His Apostolic Majesty the King-Emperor. Hungary was granted her own cabinet, and virtual autonomy in domestic affairs. Both partners in the monarchy shared an army, a navy, and finance ministry, with the emperor as their supreme commander. German was still the official tongue of army and government offices, but military orders could be given in either tongue.

The *Ausgleich* was ratified on 29 May 1867. On 8 June, Francis Joseph and Elizabeth were crowned king and queen of Hungary in a glittering ceremony such as the city of Budapest had never yet seen. The pageantry reached its climax when the king-emperor mounted his white charger, rode up Coronation Hill, and pointed the sword of Stephen towards all four points of the compass – a symbolic resolution to protect Hungary from her enemies on every border.

For the Magyars, the *Ausgleich* was a resounding victory, much as it was resented by Vienna and by minority groups – notably the Slavs and Serbs – still living within the dual monarchy's borders. For Francis Joseph, it was a concession which he accepted with praiseworthy grace. But if it was in any sense a personal humiliation for Habsburg pride, it was to be cruelly eclipsed within less than a month.

If 1866 had been an unhappy year for the dynasty, 1867 was to bring an even more crushing blow.

Those who predicted disaster for Maximilian and Carlota in Mexico were to be proved horribly correct. When the new emperor and empress landed at Vera Cruz in May 1864, there were no crowds to welcome or cheer them on their way. Both worked unstintingly in their new surroundings, Maximilian travelling throughout the country's provinces while Carlota acted as his regent to transact governmental business in his absence.

Only gradually did they realise how grossly Napoleon had misled them. Far from French troops being in control, Mexican forces were by no means held in check. Resentment at a Habsburg archduke being foisted on them ran high. When the American civil war ended, pressure on Napoleon to withdraw his troops and financial support intensified. Personal relations between the still-childless emperor and empress deteriorated, but Carlota still stood solidly by her husband after France had withdrawn her interests.

She returned to Europe in a desperate mission to beg Napoleon for help. Despite her accusations of treachery and double-dealing, he insisted he could do nothing more. From Paris she travelled to Rome, to ask the pope for help; he could offer nothing but sympathy. By now, years of tension had left their mark on Carlota. Her attendants noticed with unease the increasing moods of paranoia, and outbursts of irrational temper, and her brother Philippe, count of Flanders, was shocked at her haggard appearance and intermittent nervous energy. Before long, rumours circulating throughout Europe were confirmed. The empress of Mexico had become mentally unhinged. Queen Victoria lamented (20 October 1866) that

It is all that wretched folly of going to Mexico, which dearest Papa was so against that I think he would have prevented it, which has deranged her poor mind. She urged it, and she urged Max to go when he began to waver. And no doubt this and the failure of her attempts to procure assistance from France and elsewhere is the cause of this – added to fatigue and excitement.[17]

In her more lucid moments Carlota wrote to Maximilian, though her letters were mainly accounts of life at Miramare without him. At first hopes were entertained for her recovery, but eventually it was clear that she would only regain fitful sanity. Still only aged twenty-six and robust physically if not mentally, she was to live a twilight existence until 1927, believing herself a reigning empress and demanding gifts to be sent to England where she believed her husband was imprisoned.

In Mexico, Maximilian's situation became steadily more untenable. The remaining French military presence left in February 1867 and he bravely placed himself at the head of imperialist troops, trying to ward off the Juaristas. In May his army deserted him and transferred its allegiance to General Juarez. He surrendered, and at a court-martial was sentenced to death for treason. Two officers who had remained loyal to him to the last, Generals Miramon and Meija, were to share his fate.

The three men met their end in front of a firing squad outside Queretaro on 19 June 1867. Just before the shots rang out, Maximilian announced in Spanish that he forgave everyone, asked for forgiveness himself, and that in giving his life he sincerely hoped peace would come to Mexico.

On 1 July a telegram in cypher reached Paris, where a world fair was delighting people from all nations. Both King William of Prussia and Tsar Alexander II, neither of whom had previously had much respect for the French, were good-naturedly paying their respects. Francis Joseph had been invited and was due to arrive shortly. The highlight of this exhibition season, a prize-giving ceremony in the Palais d'Industrie, was about to take place. Napoleon burst into tears on reading the message, but quickly pulled himself together and broke the news to Eugenie. Presentations took place, but her self-control gradually gave way, and on her return to the Tuileries she was carried half-fainting to her bed. Little did the emperor and empress of the

French know that morning editions of *L'Independence Belge* already carried the tragic news.

Francis Joseph was on holiday in Bavaria with his wife and children, an almost unique occurrence, when the unhappy tidings were broken to him. Only a fortnight earlier, he had been assured by Napoleon that Maximilian's life was in no danger. He had been convinced that Mexican rebels would never dare put a Habsburg archduke to death. Full of remorse at not having forbidden his brother to go in the first place, he hurried to Vienna in order to be the first to tell their parents. The Archduchess Sophie was completely broken by her favourite son's death, weeping bitterly that savages had murdered him as if he was a common criminal.

In England, Queen Victoria received a telegram on 2 July announcing Maximilian's fate, yet it 'seemed uncertain'. She too felt unable to accept that the worst had indeed come to pass. But a second telegram on 4 July from the Austrian minister at Washington confirmed it. Next day it was in the British press. She noted in her journal that it was

> Too horrid! Poor dear unhappy Charlotte bereft of her reason, and her husband killed. What a shocking end to their luckless undertaking, which I did all I could do to prevent, and which dearest Albert was so much against.

Ironically it happened at a convenient time for Her Majesty. She had been due to review troops at Hyde Park on 5 July, in a ceremony which was to be made 'as imposing as possible' by her cousin George, duke of Cambridge and commander-in-chief of the army. Prime minister Lord Derby was aghast at her intention of taking John Brown, her personal Highland attendant. The sight of Brown, who had already fiercely divided Queen Victoria's family and given rise to much salacious gossip throughout the country, might lead to incidents of 'an unpleasant nature', he advised. 'The Queen will not be dictated to,' she retorted. Such deadlock between monarch and minister was resolved not by personal compromise, but by a realisation on both sides that it would be expedient to cancel the review as a mark of respect to the memory of the late emperor of Mexico.

With Maximilian dead and Charlotte incurably insane, an era in relations between the families of Queen Victoria and Emperor Francis Joseph came to an end. Maximilian was the only one Queen Victoria had known well, and the only one Prince Albert had ever met. Both had liked and respected him; the queen found him infinitely more approachable than his elder brother, and had Albert met the emperor too, he would have surely shared his wife's opinion.

Moreover, in his marriage to Charlotte – childless and unhappy though it may have been – an important link had been forged, albeit briefly, between the Habsburgs and Coburgs. The queen's uncle and perpetual father-figure King Leopold had died in December 1865, and with his daughter as good as dead to the world, the link was now broken. There would be further meetings between queen and emperor, as well as personal contacts between queen, empress and crown prince, but without the same degree of rapport as there had been with that most charming, imaginative and tragic archduke.

CHAPTER 4

'That singular dear Lady'

If the past belonged to Queen Victoria, the present and future belonged to Albert Edward, prince of Wales. This was certainly the view of London society in the late 1860s, bored and irritated by the spectacle of the widowed queen in her incessant mourning.

In a sense, it was also to apply to such affinity as was to exist between Windsor and Vienna for the next few decades. From his wedding in 1863 until his death in 1910 after a nine-year reign as king, the prince of Wales personified the public face of monarchy at home and abroad. Queen Victoria's obstinate seclusion proved potentially dangerous to the well-being of the institution at one stage, and although she was eventually prevailed upon to make further public appearances in her old age, notably at her jubilee celebrations in 1887 and 1897, her eldest son was far more conspicuous. While her journeys around Europe (including the four occasions on which she met Emperor Francis Joseph) were undertaken almost exclusively for family reasons, it was her successor who, by his frequent visits to crowned heads and their heirs on the continent, preserved a high profile for the British monarchy on a personal and, within limits of the crown's constitutional powers, political level.

The prince's first visit to Vienna with Princess Alexandra took place in January 1869, as they were en route to Egypt (as he had been in 1862). They had spent a family Christmas with their children and the Danish royal family at Fredensborg in Denmark. After a courtesy call to Berlin early in the new year, noted more for the rudeness of Queen Augusta of Prussia than for anything else, they found Vienna very congenial, albeit impossible for royalty to pay 'unofficial visits' to the Austrian capital. There were endless formal dinners and receptions laid on, and what was meant to be a private sojourn had been dominated by the necessity of paying courtesy calls to every member of the Habsburgs in or near Vienna. As there were twenty-seven archdukes, not to mention lesser relations, it was a time-consuming task.

Yet they were treated with more friendliness than they had been at Berlin. Francis Joseph understood the necessity of flattering England, particularly after Austria's crushing defeat by the Prussians. Prince and princess both enjoyed skating parties, ballet performances, a concert at which Johann Strauss conducted his waltzes, and a tour of the imperial stables housing five hundred horses belonging to Empress Elizabeth.

The empress apparently got on well with her husband's guests, finding that they disliked excessive protocol almost as much as she did, and being enchanted by finding in Alexandra another princess devoted to horses. Apart from this shared interest, and the fact that they were noted by contemporaries for their beauty, they had little in common.

In 1873 the prince of Wales was appointed president of the British section of the Vienna exhibition of industry and art. London had greatly impressed the world in 1851; Paris had followed her example in 1867; six years later, it was the turn of Austria's capital. New hotels, cafes and restaurants were built to cater for tourists coming from all corners of the universe, to see exhibits laid out over an area of 280 acres.

This exhibition was more than a demonstration of Austria's wealth and commercial progress in recent years. It was also intended to help prove that the Austro–Hungarian empire was still a major European power. In 1871 the German empire had been born out of the Franco-Prussian war, a conflict in which the sympathies of Francis Joseph and his ministers had secretly been with the 'arch-rogue' Napoleon. The Austrian emperor was shocked by the declaration of this new upstart empire, loathing Bismarck and detesting King (now also German Emperor) William's 'vanity and sanctimoniousness'.

Austria and England shared unease of imperial Germany as a formidable commercial and industrial rival, and in Vienna the need for friendly Anglo-Austrian relations was recognised. It was appreciated that England looked more kindly on the Habsburg empire, partly because of her new attitude towards Hungary, partly as a result of her democratic internal reforms, and partly because she might be needed as a bulwark against Russian expansion in the Balkans and middle east.

The prince of Wales and his brother Prince Arthur* attended the opening of the Vienna exhibition on 1 May 1873, as well as their sister the German crown princess and her husband. Albert Edward and Frederick William made a strange contrast, for the former was regarded as charming and affable if rather too casual, inclined to be late for appointments (which seems hard to believe, knowing how he always deprecated his wife's chronic unpunctuality at home), the

---

* Later duke of Connaught and Strathearn.

other in his military uniform a painful reminder of Austria's defeat at Königgrätz. Yet the German crown prince, who also hated Bismarck and shared his belief in the greatness of Prussia but certainly not his ultra-conservative politics, might be a useful personal ally of Austria when he eventually succeeded his aged father.

The crown princess commented with some asperity that the exhibition was only a third part ready on opening, and not nearly so striking as the Paris one. Yet, as she readily admitted, it was hard to compare it favourably with that which had been opened at the Crystal Palace exactly twenty-two years earlier. Patriotically she wrote to Queen Victoria (18 May) that her brother had

> been of great use to the English Committee, and certainly the English department has come out best, has been the best arranged, the first to be ready, and has almost the finest show of things.[1]

Although on excellent terms with the German crown prince, the prince of Wales was a little put out at learning that Frederick William had been chosen to precede him at all state banquets and receptions. He considered it an unfortunate sign that Austria was prepared to relegate herself to being Prussia's catspaw in the European hierarchy, and was hardly mollified by Francis Joseph's assurance that he maintained all foreign powers were equal at his court.

Otherwise the visit passed off pleasantly enough, notwithstanding excessive Habsburg formality to which the prince was no stranger. The empress, he wrote to Queen Victoria (2 May) was

> still very handsome and nothing can exceed her kindness and that of the Emperor towards us . . . We have been to several evening parties and are invited to dinner every day, but the early hours cut up one's day very much.[2]

He was favourably impressed by structural improvements made to Vienna since his previous visit in 1869:

> During the four years since I was here – Vienna has increased very much in size – and splendid houses are being built everywhere – and the streets widened which is very necessary – as the old ones are so narrow.[3]

With tongue in cheek, he could not resist a playful taunt concerning his younger brother, whose status as his mother's favourite son Queen Victoria made no effort to hide. Arthur, he informed her, was 'very well and has had only one headache – and I take great care that he does not tire himself'.[4]

He also met two contemporary princes of the next generation, his nephew Prince William of Germany and (for the first time) Crown Prince Rudolf, both then aged fourteen. Each was to colour his experiences as a royal ambassador to the courts of Vienna and Berlin during the next fifteen years or so in dramatically different ways. But nobody came more under his influence than the Empress Elizabeth. Much as she hated formal dinners with visiting guests, the sparkling personality and conversation of the English heir apparent made these occasions more than bearable for once. Knowing of her interest in horses and in hunting, he enchanted her with his glowing, good-humoured descriptions of sport in the shires. She listened keenly, and resolved that one day she too would go hunting in England.

After duty came pleasure for the British princes. Following ten days of functions and festivities, Edward and Arthur took a trip down the Danube to visit Hungary. They had heard much about the delights of this distant country and were determined to see it for themselves.

On 11 May they embarked at Vienna on a steamer rechristened *Ariadne* after the prince of Wales' cruising yacht. From all accounts it was a lively party with much sightseeing along the river, and they reached Budapest at eight in the evening. About 20,000 people greeted them as they stepped ashore. They dined at the national casino, Hungary's most fashionable night club, run largely along British lines. During the next few days they joined in the fun at a combined Hungarian gipsy fete and English-style regatta staged at Archduke Joseph's Margaret Island on the Danube; an opera performance followed by their first effort at the Hungarian national dance, the *Czárdás;* and, to round off the Magyar interlude, a ball in the Hotel Europa at which everyone danced until five in the morning.

The prince of Wales and Budapest each lived up to the other's expectations. He enjoyed the convivial night life and informality of all he saw and did, and the colourful, unpretentious Magyar manner impressed him as it had the shy Empress Elizabeth. The people of Budapest, knowing that Britain had long been sympathetic to Hungarian aspirations, were delighted to find in her heir to the throne a prince full of dignity but without pomposity, and one who was determined to enjoy life to the full as much as they did.

Edmund Monson, British consul-general at Budapest, summed up the visit fulsomely in a letter to Lord Granville (14 May):

> This demonstration of national sympathy for the Princes of the Royal House of Great Britain has been so unequivocally genuine and spontaneous, so universal and so persistent as to convince every Englishman and Foreigner who witnessed it of the sincerity of the oft-repeated declaration that while on the one hand the

Hungarians know that of all the European nations there is none that can vie with England in interest in their constitutional life and progress and in their efforts to maintain and develop their national freedom, so there is on the other hand no country to which they themselves are more attracted by similarity of character and habits, by identity of policy and interests, and especially by admiration of our Sovereign and of all the members of the Royal Family.[5]

In 1874 it was the empress's turn to enjoy a few days of peaceful recreation in England. Elizabeth's sympathies with the country dated back to her first flight from Vienna, when she had borrowed the yacht *Victoria and Albert* and had her desire for privacy at Malta respected. Now her sister the ex-queen of Naples was writing glowingly to her on the charm of England, the one country she had yet known where royalties were allowed to live in peace, and where hunting was excellent. This last fact was no more than confirmation of what the Prince of Wales had told her when they met at the Vienna exhibition, and she could wait no longer to see for herself.

At the end of July she took her youngest child, the six-year-old Archduchess Valerie, to the Isle of Wight. In one way this was a strange choice, for Queen Victoria was at Osborne House, and Elizabeth was not noted for responding enthusiastically to social obligations when on holiday. But the island was considered more secluded than mainland Britain, and famed for what contemporary travel guides called 'its bracing and salubrious resorts'. They went ostensibly on medical advice, for court doctors had prescribed 'invigorating sea-baths' for mother and daughter.

In reality, Elizabeth felt the need to get away from Vienna, where she was being unfairly blamed for political intrigues. Different parties and nationalist elements within the empire were accusing her of influencing the emperor at their expense, above all certain conservative and centralist groups who had been championed by the late Archduchess Sophie and who sorely missed her support.* It was seldom realised that Elizabeth had never attempted to influence her husband in political issues since the *Ausgleich* and Hungarian coronation in 1867, even though he still regularly asked her advice and respected her judgment.

On 28 July, the 'countess and Fraulein von Hohenembs' (the empress and her daughter) left Vienna and travelled to England via Strasbourg and Le Havre. Accompanied by their maids Marie Festetics and Ida

---

* The archduchess died in May 1872, broken in spirit by Maximilian's death and by the humiliation of Austria's eclipse by Bismarck's Prussia, a decline sealed by the Franco-Prussian war. The Archduke Francis outlived her by six years, dying in 1878. On hearing of her last illness, the German crown princess expressed sympathy not only for her but also for the emperor, lamenting that the archduchess's intrigues had done 'a great amount of mischief, most of all to her own son.'

Ferenczy, with a large suite of chaplains and doctors, governesses and nurses, hairdressers, masseurs, French chefs and Hungarian pastrycooks, plus the inevitable horses, carriages, grooms and trainers, they descended on the island on 2 August. Count Beust, Austrian ambassador to London, had rented Steephill Castle for them, about a mile to the west of Ventnor and commanding a magnificent sea view.

The islanders and other summer visitors had rarely seen such a stately influx of guests, and modifications carried out for them at Steephill were no secret. It was well known that the billiard room had been fitted out as a gymnasium, where the empress vaulted over wooden horses with the agility of a circus artiste, that new bathrooms had been installed, that pounds of beefsteak were pressed daily into pulp for glasses of ox-blood mixed with chicken broth, said to be her only nourishment because of her obsessive weight-watching, and that a Jersey cow was visited every morning by the vet to provide the young archduchess with milk.

Yet despite the buzz of excited chatter in local shops, and astonished stares at the army of colourful Hungarian servants, most people respected her wish for privacy. Tourists armed with binoculars would crowd neighbouring cliffs to watch her bathing, but they were hoodwinked by a maid who resembled her in height and figure. She would go into the water accompanied by a guard and lady-in-waiting, while her imperial mistress bathed privately on the other side of the island. ˙

Elizabeth adored the Gothic castle of Steephill, which reminded her of her childhood home at Possenhofen in Bavaria. She was enchanted by gardens banked profusely with myrtle, shaded with luxuriant magnolias and camellias, surrounded by rich deciduous woodland, all at their best in the magnificent summer weather.

Yet she must have known with a sinking feeling that she could not long escape the self-proclaimed 'doyenne of sovereigns', or indeed other members of the family staying at or close to Osborne. She and her suite were barely installed before Queen Victoria announced her visit. The queen was at her most gracious, and pleasantly surprised at finding the empress more normal than gossip would have had her believe. Expecting an unbalanced neurotic who was liable to drift off and sit staring out of the window or lock herself away in fits of weeping without a moment's warning, instead she found herself face to face with an apparently healthy young woman full of enthusiasm for the joys of bathing and walking and the splendours of the island scenery, as proud of her little daughter as any mother.

But from letters written afterwards by both, it was an uncomfortable experience, marked by an exchange of frigid pleasantries and little else. With a curious distortion of facts, Queen Victoria reported to the German crown princess that the empress had insisted on coming over to see her:

> We are all disappointed. A great beauty I cannot call her. She has a beautiful complexion, a splendid figure, and pretty, small eyes and not a very pretty nose.[6]

Meanwhile Elizabeth was writing to Francis Joseph that Queen Victoria was very kind, 'and said nothing that was not amiable, but she is not sympathetic to me'. The dumpy but still indomitably majestic queen in her widow's weeds unnerved the empress, whose fragile beauty could not but help emphasise how little the two women had in common. As for Valerie, she was terrified, and told her mother afterwards that she had never seen such a stout lady. The queen may have felt subconsciously a little jealous of her ethereal guest, who floated rather than walked and barely raised her voice above a modest whisper.

At a hotel in Sandown next day the empress gladly renewed her acquaintance with the German crown princess, one of the few royalties she regarded as a genuine friend. The sympathetic Crown Princess Frederick William knew only too well how it felt to live at an imperial court where intelligence and individuality were deeply resented by diehards who maintained that women, especially princesses, should have no abiding interests outside the three K's(*Kirche, Kuche, Kinder*).A letter to Queen Victoria (3 August) reveals much about the routine of Elizabeth, whom she called 'a very funny person with her arrangements':

> She sleeps a great part of the forenoon on her sofa – dines at 4 and rides the whole evening quite alone – and never for a shorter time than 3 hours and becomes frantic if anything else is proposed. She does not wish to see a soul – or show herself anywhere. All the same I like her very much and she is very kind to me.[7]

Elizabeth also saw the princess of Wales (who had been the subject of much secret comparison as to relative beauty between the two Victorias, Alexandra coming off somewhat better) and found her 'very kind, nice looking and as deaf as a post'. In later years she would always maintain that of all European royals only she and Alexandra knew how to dress. This compliment would be returned by the latter's son, King George V, who would tell his family that he was brought up in an age of beautiful women, 'and the two most beautiful of all were the Empress Elizabeth of Austria and my own mother'.[8]

To Francis Joseph, Elizabeth wrote:

> I was most polite, I may say, at which everybody seemed quite
> astonished. But now I have done my duty. They quite
> understand that I want to be quiet, and they have no wish to
> intrude.[9]

Or so she thought. A few days later Queen Victoria invited the
empress to dinner. She refused, insisting to her husband that she was
sure the queen would be glad to be relieved of making the effort, and
only admitting to her mother that 'that kind of thing bores me'. But
Her Majesty was not accustomed to being turned down in this way,
and renewed her invitation. She need not have bothered, and Elizabeth's second refusal led her to agree with her relations that the
young empress of Austria might be beautiful but totally lacking in any
sense of duty as regarding her royal obligations.

Having successfully extricated herself from the attentions of her
would-be hostess, Elizabeth left the island for a few days to enjoy
London incognito. 'Everybody is away,' she wrote happily; 'the
streets with the finest houses seem as though dead.' In other words,
there was no danger of being lionised by society hosts and hostesses in
Mayfair and Belgravia, where blinds were drawn and she could walk
around largely unrecognised. She paid a call on Francis, duke of Teck
at the White Lodge, Richmond, whom she remembered from his
army days in Austria. Now in the capital he and his duchess were
greeted as valued companions. Elizabeth was also briefly a guest at
Clarence House, where the recently-married duchess of Edinburgh
was quietly awaiting the birth of her first child.

Like many a summer visitor to London before and since, Elizabeth
could not wait to see the great sights of the metropolis. Count Beust
had to give up his own holiday and arrange her visits to places she
wanted. They entered Madame Tussaud's waxworks collection,
where she was amused to find a model of the emperor, 'so lifelike as to
be almost uncanny'. The rest of the show was 'very gruesome in
parts', though as she spent almost two hours there she obviously
relished what she saw.

One place on her list which Marie Festetics would have dearly liked
to avoid was Bedlam, Lambeth, at that time the largest lunatic asylum
in existence. Although the empress could be very selfish in her
demands on others, her compassion for the insane showed a remarkable selflessness matched by few of her station. She questioned doctors
and nurses with keen interest, and spoke to a male patient who begged
her to set him free. Gently she asked him why he was there. He replied
that the Jesuits had a grudge against him, and as an excuse for locking
him up they accused him of having stolen St Peter's purse in the street.

That would have been a serious crime, he admitted, but it was not true as he was St Peter himself. Calmly she told him that he could therefore be certain of regaining his freedom soon.

In the evenings she and Count Beust went riding in Hyde Park, she being mounted on the white horse he had ridden at the coronation in Budapest. Crowds of holidaymakers came eagerly to the railings of Rotten Row to admire this beautiful apparition clad in a white coat with gold buttons, who rode with such effortless grace. For once she did not seem to object to the attentions of so many spectators, finding the informality of London as a whole a welcome contrast to her restricted existence in Vienna.

As news spread that the empress of Austria was in the city, so did the Austrian embassy become a magnet for horse breeders offering suitable animals for sale at exorbitant prices. Predictably the choicest beasts were the most expensive. With typical feminine guile she wrote wistfully to the emperor that the one she would most like to acquire cost 25,000 gulden,'so it is naturally out of the question.' Back came an affectionate telegram authorising her to purchase whatever she liked.

Next Elizabeth went north to Melton and Belvoir Castle, estates of the duke of Rutland. On 26 August she attended the first cub-hunt of the season, rising cheerfully at dawn and spending all day in the saddle. She laughed merrily when some of her gentlemen in attendance were so worn out by the hunt that they nodded off in her presence that evening. After spending a night at Melton and visiting the stables, she felt that soon she must arrange to spend a complete hunting season there.

By coincidence, at the hunt there were several gentlemen from the Austro-Hungarian empire who followed the empress around. With some amusement she referred to them as 'her colony'. Marie Festetics did not enjoy their sojourn at Belvoir, and disapproved of the way in which English society welcomed with open arms anybody rich and sporting. Elizabeth found such moral strictures a bore, as did the prince of Wales, and appreciated being free to accept as friends anybody she met in England on these occasions, even if they belonged to social circles which made them unacceptable at the Viennese court. Indeed, the rebellious streak in her must have found perverse pleasure in bestowing her approval on such people who were not of sufficiently noble birth.

Ironically, those who incurred Marie's distrust most of all were the Baltazzi brothers. The sons of a Levantine merchant, they had entered fashionable racing society in Vienna and belonged to the hunt at Gödöllo in Hungary, through their elder sister Helene, wife of the imperial diplomat Baron Vetsera. Well might she comment thus, for fifteen years hence, the name of Vetsera would be linked with the imperial dynasty in the most horrific manner imaginable.

How Elizabeth must have cursed her destiny and wished that instead she had had the good fortune to marry into the English hunting nobility! She was quite sad to leave the green fields and well-tended stables of Leicestershire after the allotted two days and return to the Isle of Wight, but she revelled in a stormy passage across the Solent during which most of her companions were violently seasick. Looking at the tempestuous waters, she began to crave for a long ocean voyage. To her mother, she wrote that what she would like next was a short visit to America.

Yet her return to Steephill Castle was not without its compensations. Queen Victoria had gone north to Balmoral, with a friendly telegram from the 'Countess of Hohenembs' sent from Ventnor (18 August):

> I beg Your Majesty to accept my best thanks for your very amiable remembrance and all the kindness you had for me. I am very sorry not to meet Your Majesty any more on these occasions and send you my best wishes for a pleasant journey.[10]

In view of Elizabeth's refusal of her invitations, the queen must have found this second sentence rather ironic.

It was followed by another telegram from Ventnor (29 August):

> I feel very much touched by the great kindness Your Majesty has shown me and send my warmest regards for telegrams, flowers and fruit.[11]

Back at Ventnor she resumed her sea bathing for a few more days. Over-whelmed by her enthusiasm for England, she wrote impulsively to her husband regretting what a shame it was that he could not join her:

> After all those manoeuvres you might really take a fortnight off to see London, then dash up to Scotland to visit the Queen, and then have a little hunting in the neighbourhood of London. We have horses and everything here, so it would be a pity not to use them. Do think it over for a day or two before, with your usual refractoriness, you say no . . .[12]

Still she seemed unable to accept that the emperor of Austria-Hungary had planned his life well in advance, and that duty counted for more than personal pleasure. Late in September she too realised that her return home could not be postponed indefinitely. With regret she said goodbye to the Isle of Wight, returning to Vienna early the next month. From Schönbrunn (7 October) she acknowledged a message from Queen Victoria:

> I thank Your Majesty with all my heart for your kind telegram, and also for your many kindnesses during my stay in England. This morning I arrived here safely. The Emperor thanks you for your gracious remembrance and lays himself at your feet.[13]

Elizabeth's chance to spend a full hunting season in England came in March 1876. The people of Northamptonshire were thrilled to hear that the empress of Austria had rented Easton Neston for six weeks of sport. Queen Victoria was not pleased at the prospect of 'that singular dear Lady. . .really coming over here to hunt!!! I think it very unbecoming as well as dangerous. . .'[14]

This time Elizabeth, or rather Beust, had strict instructions from Francis Joseph that she was to pay her respects to Queen Victoria, and there was to be no repetition of her behaviour on the Isle of Wight. There were political motives behind his reasoning, for England and Austria-Hungary were united over the Eastern question, although he was still trying to negotiate with Tsar Alexander for a friendly solution to the Balkan problem.

Elizabeth therefore stopped in London on her way to Northamptonshire, but the queen was determined to extract a gentle measure of revenge after what had happened before. She sent word that she was too busy to receive the empress at present, but looked forward to doing so at some later date. Rather piqued but not without a sense of guilt, she spent an extra day at London in order to receive the Tecks, Waleses and Edinburghs, making a conscious effort to be charming to each. 'Imagine if I were so ill-bred,' she wrote to her husband after the queen's refusal. 'But everybody whom I visited this afternoon was ashamed, for I made myself very agreeable.'[15]

At Easton Neston, Elizabeth was delighted at the extensive stabling, large parks, and above all an opportunity to hunt with several different packs. Within a day of her arrival she was already at a meet. Lord Spencer, squire of Althorp and master of the Pytchley hunt, appointed Captain George 'Bay' Middleton to pilot her during her first hunting season. At first he was unimpressed, saying scornfully, 'What is an empress to me?' But he changed his mind after seeing that the empress was not only just as charming as popular legend made out, but also a keen and fearless horsewoman.

With ill-concealed reluctance, Elizabeth sent word that she would visit Queen Victoria at Windsor on Sunday 12 March. It was evident that she intended to stay there for the least time possible. She declined an invitation to spend a night at the castle, and allowed several conflicting messages to be sent as to whether she would stay for luncheon or not. Neither queen nor court approved of Sunday visiting. Elizabeth must have known, and found malicious satisfaction in knowing what a furore this would cause.

Before divine service at Windsor (starting at midday), the bishop of Peterborough was informed that Her Majesty commanded him on no account to preach a long sermon. She might have spared herself the trouble. Just as he was mounting the steps of his pulpit, a page entered the church and whispered that the empress of Austria's arrival was imminent. Elizabeth could not have timed it better (or worse from Queen Victoria's point of view) if she had tried. The queen stumped down crossly to the chapel door to receive her difficult guest. There was a flurry of presentations and introductions. By this time it was snowing, and the empress seized on this as a perfect excuse for not staying to luncheon. Her visit thus lasted a mere three quarters of an hour. The queen noted in her journal rather acidly that her visitor spoke of nothing but hunting, and how civil everyone was – in other words, everyone in her sporting circles. It was not a gesture calculated to improve relations between the ruling houses.

If Elizabeth smiled quietly to herself on having showed Queen Victoria how much the court at Windsor and the whole concept of ceremonial etiquette bored her, divine retribution was not long in coming. The train bearing her and her suite back to London broke down in the snow. She ordered the station-master to bring her luncheon and a bottle of claret in her carriage.

As if to draw attention to her indiscretions, on the Monday she paid a full and formal visit to Ferdinand de Rothschild. Hunting was impossible because of the snow, but she called on him at Leighton House and they rode over to inspect his stud at Mentmore. Such tactlessness must have infuriated the queen, whose reaction can easily be imagined.

Once the weather had cleared Elizabeth was back in the saddle, attending every hunt she could, and disappointed that she could not participate in them all.

To her husband, she wrote that she had not felt a moment's fatigue since arrival, and was 'as tanned as a wild hare'. Considering that spring had barely arrived and she had been held up by heavy snow only a few days previously, this description seems rather exaggerated. Those who had feared she had only months if not weeks to live during the dark times of 1860–61 would have hardly recognised her as the same person.

She loved being in England, finding the people amusing and friendly, treating her neither with fawning obeisance nor disrespect or impatient criticism. When told that only four of her horses were fit to be ridden over English countryside the way she rode them, she accepted the judgment without question, and wrote back ungratefully to the emperor that 'his horses' were no good; they were too slow and spiritless. In turn, others found her dignified yet with delightful girlish näiveté, genuinely grateful for the slightest kindness shown her. The queen of Naples was considered too arrogant and was never really popular in England, but her imperial sister was greatly admired and loved by those in the shires with whom she came into contact. Even the Austrians in her 'colony' seemed to behave in a more human, less artificial fashion in England than in Vienna. The dinner parties every evening were grand lavish affairs, but far less formal than tedious banquets at the Hofburg. It was a pleasant change sitting down to dine and enjoy lively humorous conversation, to recall the day's events, and for Elizabeth to receive compliments on her beauty and sporting prowess rather than pious empty flatteries accorded to her as first lady of the empire.

It was a wrench to say goodbye to the shires and her friends when April came, and she had to return home.

Less than two years later, Crown Prince Rudolf made his first visit to England. He was sent to study political and economic conditions in Britain for a couple of months. Parliamentary government in Austria was still in its infancy, and although the emperor was suspicious of this democratic institution which curtailed his autocratic powers, he was persuaded to see the value of sending his son and heir to see and hear the mother of parliaments at work. Britain was also the world's primary economic power, while Austrian industrialisation was a relatively new phenomenon.

A financial crisis in 1873, following the 'Black Friday' of the Vienna stock exchange, had dealt imperial industry a heavy blow, and recovery was only gradual. Yet growth of industry was a perquisite in Austria's remaining a major power, particularly in the light of German competition.

The idea of sending Rudolf to England so he could study the country's institutions at close range originated, it seems, with the empress. Not, it must be said, through an overwhelming concern for his education and experience, but more through her own desire to return to the shires. Choosing her moment carefully, she suggested to the emperor that Rudolf's preparation as his successor would hardly be complete without a visit to see the country's expanding economic power at first hand. It would be politic, she added, for her to accompany Rudolf – and maybe go hunting there again. Preoccupied with affairs of state, Francis Joseph gave his consent without a second thought.

Rudolf had grown up an intelligent and precocious child. As an adolescent he had filled his diary with personal thoughts which would have astonished, even shocked his elders. He was openly critical of church and aristocracy, and of the way they had comported themselves since the middle ages. To him the execution of King Louis XVI, Queen Marie Antoinette and members of the French nobility during the revolution were rough punishment, but at the same time 'a necessary and salutary catastrophe'. Perceptively he believed that monarchy, in having lost its old power, now clung to the trust and love of the people; it was a mighty ruin which would soon tumble. He had the stirrings of a social conscience, and learnt enough from his liberal tutors to sympathise instinctively with the labouring classes who worked so hard for very low wages. At the same time he was highly strung, prone (like his late uncle Maximilian) to sudden changes of mood, and a very lonely child, having little contact with children his own age. More disturbingly, he showed an unhealthy preoccupation with death, suicide and 'life on the other side', and there was evidence that he became venereally infected at the age of eighteen.

After a family Christmas in Vienna at the end of 1877, Rudolf and his mother set out for England together. With the former travelled his master of household, Count Carl Bombelles (a former servant of Maximilian, and one who had supported him faithfully in Mexico), his aide-de-camp Major Joseph van Eschenbacher, and his tutor Professor Menger.

The journey to England was not a happy one. Although mother and son were very alike in character, they felt ill at ease with each other. Writing to their cousin Ludwig, king of Bavaria, soon after their arrival in London, Rudolf complained that she spent most of her time in her own compartment on the train as she was not well. He saw through her excuses, recognising that she preferred the company of her retinue. When she did deign to see him, it was to ask for his word that he would not hunt in England. He was a poor horseman, and she did not wish her riding reputation to be tarnished by his clumsiness as a sportsman. Deeply sensitive to her criticisms, he replied that he would indeed avoid riding to hounds on English soil. There was nothing heroic in breaking one's neck as the result of such an activity. His popularity, he announced disdainfully, meant too much to him that he should risk losing it in such a foolish fashion.

As the visit was unofficial, Rudolf was not lodged at the Austro-Hugarian embassy in Belgrave Square. Instead he stayed at a hotel in Brook Street. Unlike his mother, he did not need to be told twice that he must pay a courtesy call on Queen Victoria, and he made an excellent impression, as her letter to the prince of Wales (12 January 1878) revealed:

> The young Crown Prince left us today and I am much pleased with him. He, as *all* Austrians, is most easy to get on with . . .

almost as soon as he arrived I invited him, anxious to shew all possible civility and respect to the Emperor and Empress of Austria. He is very pleasing, but looks a little over grown and *not* very robust. . .[16]

The duchess of Teck jokingly told Count Beust that Queen Victoria was quite in love with the crown prince, 'but do not worry, she does not want to marry him'. There was obviously something about the sensitive, imaginative Wittelsbach temperament, absent in Francis Joseph but noticeable in Maximilian and now Rudolf, which touched a chord in the queen's heart. Nonetheless she declined the prince of Wales's recommendation that she should confer the Order of the Garter on her guest, on the grounds that at nineteen he was too young for such an honour.

The prince of Wales and Crown Prince Rudolf had much in common. They shared political ideals to a certain extent, though Rudolf was more of a free-thinker and more intense in his convictions than the easy-going Albert Edward. Both were also deeply suspicious of Bismarck's Germany, albeit for different reasons. The prince of Wales already knew much about the offhand treatment by Bismarck and Emperor William of the Crown Prince and Princess Frederick William, whereas Rudolf had nursed a deep-rooted grievance against Prussia since the traumatic experience of Königgrätz and subsequent loss of Austrian prestige. But even at this early stage they shared profound misgivings about the arrogance of Prince William, who showed signs of growing up in the old Prussian mould, quite unlike his enlightened parents.

Rudolf had ample opportunity to meet and observe leading political personalities of the day. At a dinner party given by the prince of Wales, he and the prime minister Disraeli were guests of honour. On one of his visits to the houses of Parliament, he heard Gladstone, leader of the opposition, speak about the Oriental question. Rudolf's English was not good enough for him to understand every word, but he was impressed with the liveliness of the debate, and the blunt yet courteous exchange of views between members on both sides of the house.

Both he and Menger were so enthusiastic about British parliamentary democracy that while in Britain they collaborated on a pamphlet, *The Austrian Nobility and its Constitutional Profession : a Warning to Aristocratic Youth from an Austrian*, published anonymously in Munich later that year. In this they argued that the nobility was an important element in the stability of society, but those who were privileged enough to belong to it had a patriotic duty to prepare themselves for the posts they were to hold. Devoting themselves entirely to the enjoyment of life was insufficient, and threatened their survival in a changing world; the aristocracy must consider it an honour to serve their country and others less fortunate. They were inspired by the eminently sensible balance of British Conservatism and Liberalism, with each party alternating in government and opposition. The publication angered court circles, and many correctly suspected the true identity of its imperial co-author.

Yet Rudolf was not intimidated. He continued to nurse the prospect of Liberals from all nations throughout the Austro-Hungarian empire merging into a supranational Liberal party, and a parallel organisation of all Conservatives. In this way the imperial parliament would comprise two main parties whose basic political principles would be unsullied by differences in their fight to maintain Austria-Hungary's position as a leading European power.

Rudolf's programme in England had been carefully worked out by Herr Scherzer, commercial counsellor at the Austrian embassy in London. His brief was for the crown prince to see 'how the immensely increasing population of London was governed, fed and educated'; 'how a trade which reaches beyond the limits of the civilised world' was maintained, and 'those industrial establishments which by trying to satisfy the needs of the masses form the main sources of national wealth'.

With this in mind he visited the Bank of England, Smithfield and Billingsgate markets, the Corn Exchange, law courts, factories, old peoples' homes and military establishments in the capital. At the British Museum he was fascinated by the science departments, and gratified when experts he spoke to complimented him on his knowledge of such subjects. Later he toured industrial cities such as Birmingham, Liverpool, Manchester, Bradford and Sheffield, inspecting buildings of general interest and municipal developments and undertakings. At Sheffield he watched armour plate being manufactured for the Austrian government, and was presented with a hunting knife. Crossing the Irish Sea, he visited shipyards at Belfast, and was invited to a hunt near Dublin with the Ward Union staghounds. Although declining an offer to participate, he followed from the safety of a hack car.

At this time, old fortifications were being destroyed in Vienna, and replaced by the Ringstrasse. With an expanding population caused by incipient industrialisation and the movement of more country people into the city, new municipal enterprise was needed to keep Vienna's administration in line with necessary rebuilding. It was important that the future emperor of Austria-Hungary should have an opportunity of observing such developments closely in another country.

Interspersed between these study tours were rests at country seats where he could have time to consider and make detailed notes on

the impressions he gathered. From Chester he wrote to his old tutor
Latour (27 January):

> England has far exceeded my expectations; so far I am greatly
> satisfied with my journey and really enthusiastic about England,
> without failing to recognise the grave and very obvious drawbacks
> of the country. Life here is magnificent and I strive to get to know as
> much as possible. [17]

When he left England at the end of February, he was firmly converted
to her way of life, her national institutions and political system.

Elizabeth had a less successful time in England that winter. After a
perfunctory series of royal visits, she went to Northamptonshire, where
her secretary had rented Cottesbrook Hall. Despite a happy reunion with
her hunting friends, and a few enjoyably hectic days of sport, the sojourn
was spoiled by gossip about her apparent devotion to Captain
Middleton.

The relationship between them had its parallels in that between Queen
Victoria and John Brown. Middleton was not at all intimidated by
having to pilot an empress; when she took what he considered to be
unnecessary risks in the field, he spoke roughly to her. This spontaneous
plain speaking amused her, accustomed as she was to sycophantic
courtiers, but her entourage was horrified at such gross discourtesy. The
queen of Naples warned her privately that it was unwise to be seen so
much in the company of a man who was engaged to the daughter of a
local hunt master. With typical obstinacy, Elizabeth ignored her advice.

This was to have unfortunate consequences. On a previous hunting
season the queen of Naples, impressed by Middleton's skill and her
sister's praises, had sent an indirect message asking the captain if he
would pilot her. Angered at what amounted to a virtual command,
Middleton snapped that he was hanged if he was going to pilot every
damned queen who came to England. Though his refusal was couched in
somewhat less peremptory terms, it was inevitable that Marie should
learn his exact words sooner or later. The bold captain had made an
enemy for life.

She never forgave this slight, and Elizabeth's haughty disregard of her
well-meant warnings was the last straw. Shortly before Rudolf left
London for Lanarkshire to shoot with the prince of Wales and the duke of
Hamilton, he lunched privately at Eaton Place with his aunt and her
husband. Over the meal, Marie maintained her reputation for gossip and
mischief-making. By the time he travelled to Scotland, Rudolf knew
only too well what society was saying about the empress and the captain.

Soon after his return to London, at the end of a day in which he had
received a deputation of prominent Hungarians, visited the Royal

Academy, lunched with the prince and princess of Wales at Marlborough House and dined at the Turf Club, Rudolf attended a ball given by the German ambassador at Carlton House Terrace. So far, his British sojourn had been a tremendous success. Like his mother, he revelled in being treated more as an intelligent human being than a virtual deity, and was finding life far less artificial than in Vienna. There can be no doubt that all this had gone to his head. Equally, it is certain that he cared little for the empress's hunting cronies, particularly the one whose apparent liaison with her seemed to be making her – and by implication her own son as well – something of a laughing-stock in English society.

Several of the sporting set were also at the ball, and one of them introduced the crown prince and Captain Middleton. Little did he know what he had started. Drawing himself up to his full height, Rudolf stared coldly at him without saying a word, before turning his back and walking away.

If Rudolf had deliberately calculated this public insult, it was one of the most formidable of his English successes. Other guests were astonished when they realised what had happened. Middleton took it like a gentleman, as if nothing had occurred, but the event quickly found its way into society tittle-tattle. Inevitably it got back, perhaps embellished with more interesting exaggerations, to Elizabeth herself. She was deeply wounded and angered that her son could humiliate her thus. Too proud and yet too uncertain of herself to reprimand him personally and try to clear the air between them, she deliberately avoided him.

It was part of Rudolf's tragedy that the empress, whose imaginative and sensitive personality had suffered from the excessively hidebound conventions of Viennese court life, could not see how much he had taken after her, and would not give him the moral encouragement and sympathy he so needed. Such an incident might have resulted in a fierce argument between mother and son, with reconciliation following, thus strengthening the bond between them. In fact the opposite happened. Rudolf became one of many who learnt from bitter experience that hers was not a forgiving nature. She never forgave nor forgot his behaviour.

After this, the attractions of English society paled for Elizabeth. She no longer felt contented in an atmosphere where her every action was watched and misconstrued, and where gossips were eager to misinterpret harmless relationships with her friends. The fan she kept to hide her face from suspicious glances of others was used more and more. For once, she was not sorry to return to Vienna, from where she telegraphed to Queen Victoria (24 February):

> Am much obliged to Your Majesty for the kind enquiry concerning my return home. Same went quickly and thank God safely. It

gives me greatest pleasure that Rudolf earned Your Majesty's approbation, and has won such very favourable opinions. I commend him to Your Majesty's continued good will. . .[18]

As a result of a curious and possibly false incident, both Rudolf and his father appear to have been united in their admiration of Disraeli. Although facts are incomplete, the matter dated back to the Russo-Turkish war.

In 1875 the Ottoman provinces of Bosnia and Herzegovina rebelled against oppressive Turkish rule, and unrest spread to Bulgaria the following year. Russia, still smarting from defeat in the Crimean war, used this as an excuse to declare war against Turkey with the ultimate aim of creating a more powerful empire incorporating a Slavic federation in the Balkans, with their capital at Constantinople. As ever, Russian expansionist ambitions ran directly against British interests in seeing Turkey as a barrier between Russia and the Mediterranean. Within a few months, Russia conquered Turkey. The treaty of San Stefano, signed in March 1878, ceded a large area of territory to Russia. In Britain, Disraeli and Salisbury insisted that Europe could not recognise the treaty as it stood, and a congress was summoned at Berlin to discuss the Eastern problem. At the conference in June and July 1878, Russia was forced to relinquish her claims to a large part of the territory; the independence of Serbia, Roumania and Bulgaria was confirmed; England was allowed to take possession of Cyprus; and Austria was permitted to occupy Bosnia and Herzegovina, as a reward for 'assuming benevolent neutrality' during the war.

In 1879 the Austrian ambassador Count Münster visited Disraeli at Hughenden, his home in Buckinghamshire, supposedly with the secret offer of an alliance with Germany and Austria-Hungary, as Russia was preparing to attack Austria in revenge. Münster later suggested such an alliance to Bismarck, saying that the idea had come from Disraeli.

The evidence is incomplete, but whether true or not, it had a strange parallel in an episode during the British general election of spring 1880. Gladstone, who had been leader of the Liberal opposition during the previous parliament, said in his Midlothian campaign that there was nowhere on the map of Europe where one could point to and say 'there Austria did good'. Münster was angered at this comment on his master's Balkan policy, and in Britain it was rumoured that as a result Emperor Francis Joseph had openly expressed his wish that Disraeli would be returned to power at the election. Gladstone did not attempt to hide his fury, but after an overwhelming victory he was persuaded by Lord Granville to write a letter for publication withdrawing words which he had spoken on slender evidence while 'in a position of greater freedom and less responsibility.' Gladstone did so reluctantly, but refused to publish his letter until receiving private assurances from Münster that Austria had no further expansionary aims in the Balkans.

During the winter of 1878, Elizabeth became increasingly restless again. Her boredom with Vienna was nothing new, but for the first time she was openly dissatisfied with hunting in Hungary. Middleton and Spencer had fired her with enthusiasm for sport in Ireland, describing it to her as 'a huntsman's paradise' and adding that sport in the English shires was nothing by comparison. Lord Langford's house in County Meath, Summerhill, was therefore rented for a six-week stay in the new year.

It was a remarkable suggestion for Spencer, a former viceroy of Ireland, to make. Of all people, he must surely have known the effect that the empress's visit would have on Anglo-Austrian relations. Home rule for Ireland was becoming an increasingly contentious issue; it was supported wholeheartedly by Gladstone, who had indeed appointed Spencer as viceroy in his previous administration. That a reigning Catholic empress should make such a well-publicised foray to Ireland for the purpose of pleasure, thus implying solidarity with the cause of Irish independence, was tantamount to a gross insult to Queen Victoria.

The queen was aware that problems which beset the British crown in Ireland were similar to those difficulties experienced by Austria in Hungary. She had an abiding contempt for the Irish. Early in her reign she had expressed sympathy for oppressed Irish tenants, and appreciated the gulf between Catholics and Protestants. Because of this, she had supported financial aid to a Catholic seminary at Maynooth on the grounds that an educated priesthood must surely lead to a closer understanding between England and Ireland.

Such hopes did not last long. Later events only reinforced her distrust of the emerald isle. After the prince consort's death, she presented statues of him to several cities throughout the British Isles. One of these was Dublin, but the mayor and corporation had no compunction in returning this unsolicited gift to sender. Such an insult to the memory of her beloved angel was compounded by the attempted assassination of their second son Alfred, Duke of Edinburgh, in March 1868. He was visiting Australia as part of a grand royal tour of the more far-flung British possessions, and at a charity luncheon in Sydney he was shot and gravely wounded by a Fenian sympathiser. He soon recovered, but it only served to colour the queen's views on Ireland.

It seems remarkable that the visit was not forbidden by Francis Joseph, normally so sensitive to such considerations where other crowned heads were involved. During one of his regular visits to Gödöllo, Lord Spencer had assured him that news of political discontent in Ireland was greatly exaggerated by the English press, but this appears to have counted for less than the emperor's chivalrous reluctance to refuse his wife anything.

The vexed question of whether to accord this tactless personality any welcome onto English soil did not arise for Queen Victoria. At Windsor the court was in mourning for her second daughter Alice, grand duchess of Hesse, who had succumbed to diphtheria in December 1878, and also engrossed in preparations for the duke of Connaught's wedding in March 1879. Moreover Karolyi had been instructed by Vienna that the empress did not wish to break her journey in London. No official reception was forthcoming on her arrival at Dover, where she was met only by Count and Countess Karolyi and lunched privately with them at the Lord Warden hotel. As the imperial train reached Holyhead, the station doors were locked and all approaches guarded by police to prevent any spontaneous demonstration of welcome.

All was very different when Elizabeth sailed into Dublin on the steamer *Shamrock*. The mayor and corporation, and several members of the railway company, were on the platform awaiting her arrival. By the time she boarded a special train for Summerhill, a large enthusiastic crowd was waiting and cheering.

Along the entire distance of her route to Kilcock, people cheered the imperial train. At the station a red carpet was laid down to lead her to her carriage. The Austrian flag fluttered in welcome from the station mast and on the footbridge flew a green flag bearing a gold harp and the inscription 'Erin cordially welcomes the Empress'. Outside the station was a triumphal arch of evergreens into which was worked the traditional Hibernian welcome *Cead Mile Failthe* (A hundred thousand welcomes). Thick snow on the ground as she drove to Summerhill did not deter country villagers in their thousands from lining the road to wave. At the county boundary another triumphal arch beckoned her with the words 'Welcome to Royal Meath'. It was hardly the most private of visits.

On her instructions, much preparation had taken place at Summerhill to make it suitable for the accommodation of herself and her suite. One room had been converted into a temporary private chapel. A telegraph had been installed with a private line to the continent, so that messages need not be routed through England.

Elizabeth made a half-hearted effort to appease her conscience by sending Queen Victoria a hasty letter, the perfunctory nature of which can have hardly done herself (or the standing of Austria) much good (22 February 1879):

> I am promptly using the first day of my presence in Ireland in order to inform Your Majesty of my arrival and also of my intention, to

preserve the strictest incognito while acquainting myself with the peculiarities of hunting in Ireland.

Out of respect for the great pain that has befallen Your Majesty's loving, maternal, heart, I did not want to inconvenience you with my visit and, pressed for time, I hastened here. The Emperor asked me to give you his devoted respects. Rudolf kisses your hand and gratefully remembers the particular kindness which Your Majesty showed towards him. Finally I commend myself with devotion to the continued sisterly benevolence of Your Majesty.[19]

Ireland lived up to her expectations. The countryside was enchanting, and as much of the land was untilled and used for breeding cattle, pastures were surrounded by high hedges for jumping. As a result the hunting was much more hazardous. Elizabeth found the element of danger exciting, but Marie Festetics was continually frightened by risks her mistress was taking every day. She complained that never before had she heard of so many broken limbs, because of the deep ditches and Irish walls. During each hunt she saw several people being carried injured off the field.

Despite having her own private chapel at Summerhill, the empress could not resist another extraordinarily tactless gesture. On the Sunday after her arrival, she drove over to Maynooth College with two members of her suite, plus Captain Middleton, to attend mass. Maynooth, where Irish priests had been educated, was regarded in England as the centre of high popery in the British Isles, and a hotbed of sedition to boot. After mass the imperial group were guided round the college, where students cheered them warmly and were granted a free day in return.

This happened at a doubly unfortunate time. There were rumours that another outbreak of Fenian violence was to come, directed against the authorities in England. Moreover the Irish special branch, formed specially to fight the Fenian menace, had been warned by an informer that Kossuth had promised the movement his support if an uprising took place. Kossuth had lived in exile for many years in the United States, where Irish immigrants had founded the Irish Republican Movement, later the Fenian Movement. That the empress of Austria-Hungary was known throughout Europe as the Hungarians' champion, and that she had fondly compared Ireland and the Irish with her beloved Magyars, was too much of a coincidence for the English government and court.

It was something of a relief to all when Elizabeth received a telegram on 20 March containing bad news from home. The town of Szegedin in Hungary was partially destroyed by flooding, and she rose nobly to the occasion. There was no greater sacrifice she could make for the Magyars than to come home immediately, hoping to seize the urgency of the occasion as an excuse for not stopping in London on the way back to Dover and thence Vienna, in order to visit stricken areas and help victims financially. In the end she was obliged to stop at Addison Road station, Kensington, where the prince of Wales wished to pay her a courtesy visit. They met for fifteen minutes, a short and unsatisfactory encounter enjoyed by neither.

In February 1880 Elizabeth returned to Summerhill. Not even the worsening political situation could dissuade her. Agrarian unrest in Ireland had threatened to curtail hunting, and several packs were on the point of disbanding. Summerhill and the Meath were close to the disaffected area. Nationalist leader Charles Stewart Parnell had gone to the United States to raise funds for the independence movement.

Queen Victoria was astonished that the emperor should permit his wife to make yet another visit which could only jeopardise Anglo-Austrian relations. That the empress should be not merely free to go to a country where the English royal family was barely tolerated, but be positively welcomed there, was humiliating. It was inevitable that Parnell would make capital out of Elizabeth's presence, thus inferring to the Americans that Irish nationalism had Habsburg support. But it would hardly have done for British ambassadors in courts abroad to acknowledge their problems with Ireland, beyond veiled murmurings within the inner circles of court and diplomacy. The court of St James, therefore, had to swallow its pride. In any case, Francis Joseph was too preoccupied with the aftermath of the Russo-Turkish war and its implications for the Austro-German alliance to concern himself with matters which merely impinged on British prestige.

Once back in Ireland, Elizabeth hunted more recklessly still. One day she took what an experienced observer called the highest jump he had ever seen in Ireland, and her horse was pulling so badly that her hands were sore from the chafing of the reins. Yet she was still in at the kill, and afterwards called it 'the best run of the season'. Although Francis Joseph must have been pleased to know that she had found true contentment and happiness somewhere, even if it was far away from him, her letters describing hair-raising escapes from injury were hardly calculated to reassure him of her safety.

'The great advantage of Ireland,' she remarked, 'is that it has no Royal Highnesses.' But soon she had to recognise the disadvantages. The 'wonderful days' she spent there and which she would always remember, she told Lord Langford, were drawing to a close. As it was impracticable for her to keep up the lease at Summerhill indefinitely, her secretary Linger was charged with finding a suitable residence in Ireland, an equivalent to her Hungarian paradise at Gödöllo. Fortunately the Irish special branch of the British intelligence service heard of these intentions almost at once. It was reported to London that this scheme was quite intolerable, and Francis Joseph was accordingly notified.

His wife's regular riding expeditions in Ireland, he understood, had already caused quite enough embarrassment to the Austrian and British governments. The idea that she should have a residence of her own there was taking matters too far. He was anxious to establish good relations with Russia, now that Andrassy had resigned as foreign minister, to be succeeded by the Russophil Count Taaffe. Knowing that Britain was perpetually suspicious of Russia's intentions towards India, he did not wish to make an enemy of her. Elizabeth's presence in Ireland was more than a nuisance, it was about to assume proportions that could threaten the security of his empire. This was a far more pressing consideration than her temporary happiness. He issued immediate instructions that she was to leave Ireland forthwith, and pay a courtesy call on Queen Victoria before returning to Vienna. Meekly she obeyed, realising that if he had been driven to issuing such orders he obviously meant what he said.

Before saying goodbye to the emerald isle, Elizabeth indulged herself in one last day of hunting. To Lord Langford, she confided that Summerhill was the only place on earth where she had been allowed to live her life in her own way. As she left the estate, people cheered her in the streets so enthusiastically that the English viceroy felt it was intended as a deliberate insult to Queen Victoria.

Under the circumstances, this next meeting between queen and empress at Buckingham Palace could not have been anything but strained. Rather acidly the queen informed her eldest daughter (12 March 1880) that the empress was

> most amiable. She is a little aged, but still very handsome and graceful and distinguished looking and the figure beautiful, only her dress was so tight she could hardly move or sit down. [20]

Queen Victoria could never be described as vain, but this combination of feminine beauty and Catholicism, given the Anglo-Irish background, could not escape without some measure of criticism. Nonetheless Elizabeth had some consolation when she paid a visit to the prince and princess of Wales at Marlborough House. At her request she was shown the stables, said to be among the most modern in Europe.

While staying at Claridge's, Elizabeth attended a luncheon party given by Disraeli, whom she found 'hideously ugly, but interesting and entertaining'. On her return to the hotel she received a telegram. As she opened and read it, she went so pale that Marie Festetics asked what had happened. In a shaking voice, the empress told her that crown prince was engaged to Princess Stephanie of Belgium.

To Marie's remark that she was grateful it was not news of some great disaster, Elizabeth answered nervously that she prayed it would not turn out to be one.

CHAPTER 5

'The catastrophe'

Francis Joseph considered it was time for his son to marry and produce an heir. The future crown princess of Austria-Hungary had to be a Catholic of equal or similar standing to the Habsburgs, and this severely limited his choice. Rudolf was introduced to a princess from Saxony, but declined her on the grounds that she was too fat. The infanta of Spain was too ugly for him, and only one more was left – Princess Stephanie of Belgium, daughter of King Leopold II.

After diplomatic overtures from the Austrian ambassador at Brussels, Count Chotek, Rudolf visited the city in March 1880. King Leopold was one of the most hated monarchs of his time; Queen Victoria and the prince of Wales both loathed him because of his dissolute personal life and barbaric treatment of his family. Nevertheless he knew how to charm and impress his guests when it suited him, and his prospective son-in-law was quite deceived by his guile. Carried away by the charm of this apparently happy family circle, Rudolf proposed to Stephanie and was accepted.

Leopold, he wrote warmly to Latour, (11 March), was 'one of the most intelligent, cleverest and wisest men, and one of the best orators I have ever seen'. The king had certainly taken pains to be on his best behaviour. Stephanie was 'a real angel, a faithful good being who loves me, a very clever, well educated and able companion for this life who will stand by my side well and successfully in all my difficult tasks'.[1]

At the time Stephanie was only fifteen, a rather badly-educated (despite her suitor's belief to the contrary) immature tomboy. Knowing she was Rudolf's intellectual inferior, she hid her inferiority complex behind a mask of aggression which ill-suited her future prospects, while her poor sense of dress and gauche behaviour made the contrast more painful. As she was so young, there was reason to hope that with maturity all these faults could be modified, but it was not an encouraging start.

News of the engagement was received warmly in Austria and Belgium. Francis Joseph in his unimaginative way professed himself delighted at his son's choice, dismissing Elizabeth's misgivings with the bland retort that she worried too much. For the empress had the foresight to appreciate that Stephanie was too frivolous and stupid to make a good wife for her brilliant yet highly-strung son. Though these considerations were undoubtedly coloured by personal dislike and a feeling that 'nothing good' could come out of Belgium after the sad precedent of Charlotte, she proved that she was a surer judge of character than her husband. It was extremely unfortunate that she made no attempt to challenge the decision and prevent a second ill-starred Habsburg–Coburg alliance.

The wedding had to be postponed twice because Stephanie was still physically incapable of motherhood. By the time the event was arranged for 10 May 1881, and guests were arriving in Vienna, Rudolf was in a pitifully nervous condition. The long months of waiting, and a realisation that this unsophisticated girl was not his ideal partner, were telling on him. He was noticeably overwrought and depressed. The emperor, always an indifferent judge of character at the best of times, failed or refused to notice that anything was wrong. As for the empress, who could have offered him some sympathy, she disassociated herself completely from any wedding preparations.

Among guests at the ceremony was the prince of Wales. Both princes saw little of each other in private; had they done so, the elder man might have given the unhappy young bridegroom something of the reassurance he so plainly needed. The prince of Wales stayed at a hotel, as he wanted freedom to receive and accept hospitality from members of the Austrian Rothschild family without embarrassing the emperor. Rudolf was one of the few archdukes who did not spurn the Rothschilds' company.

The penultimate decade of the nineteenth century in Europe was notable for its triumvirate of imperial crown princes and their mutual rapport.

In England the prince of Wales, despite his frustration at being continually refused useful employment in affairs of state or access to official documents, enjoyed a hectic existence of social and diplomatic engagements at home and abroad. His liaisons sometimes landed him in serious trouble, but Queen Victoria always stood loyally by him though she did not condone his behaviour, and when they disagreed on various matters he earned her grudging respect by his robust yet tactful manner of standing up to her. Despite having to wait until he was nearly sixty and in indifferent health before he ascended the throne, he was undoubtedly the most contented of the three. His basically cheerful, easy-going temperament and zest – one might say lust – for life helped him to accept with some equanimity a situation that more sensitive princes would have found deeply mortifying.

Far less fortunate were his close friends and fellow-heirs on the continent. In Austria, Crown Prince Rudolf lived eternally in the shadow of his father, who distrusted him and (as with Queen Victoria and her son) obstinately denied him any share in statecraft. Unlike Prince Albert Edward, he had no house of his own, very little money, and even if he had had the private means, was forbidden to travel outside the Austro-Hungarian empire without the monarch's express permission. Moreover, he was temperamentally incapable of standing up to his father. Though he had showed early promise of being a man of vision and reforming instinct who took his future inheritance and politics seriously ('When I am Emperor. . .'), his extreme frustration and unhappy marriage to a shallow-minded princess who could not or would not understand his complicated character was driving him into a life of unbridled excess. The less vulnerable prince of Wales knew where to draw the line as far as pleasures of the flesh were concerned. Rudolf did not.

In Germany, Crown Prince Frederick William was barely on speaking terms with his senile father, and was treated with contempt by the imperial chief minister. Bismarck feared with good reason the liberalising, democratic ideals the prince had inherited from his mother the Empress Augusta, and which had been fortified by untiring support from his vivacious wife. Almost without exception, their personal household staff and servants were spies who had been chosen and carefully primed by Bismarck to report on activities, conversations and thoughts of the crown prince and princess. Even their 'private' correspondence and diaries were not safe from prying eyes, and many of their friends and allies in public life paid dearly for their support for the future German emperor.

Of the three princes, Frederick William seemed destined – as indeed he was – to be the one who had least time to wait. The Emperor William was approaching his ninetieth birthday, and could not be expected to live much longer. But endless years of waiting had left their mark on his son, who was frequently unwell during winter, and suffered from moods of intense depression. In his more melancholy moments he told family and friends that he believed he would never rule; the succession would skip a generation.

Bismarck was equally suspicious of all three monarchs-in-waiting. He had met Rudolf on several occasions since the latter's return from England in 1878, and even then suspected that he had discussed with the prince of Wales a possible alliance between Austria, England and France, and renewal of the Austro-Russian alliance. This threat to encircle the German empire was a deeply disturbing one. Through his network of espionage, Bismarck knew that Rudolf held strong Francophil sympathies which verged on heresy. Rudolf regarded France and her survival since the Franco-Prussian war as proof that European republics could 'perform great tasks':

> We are indebted to France as the source of all liberal ideas and constitutions in Europe. And whenever great ideas begin to ferment, France will be looked to for an example. What is Germany compared to her? Nothing but an enormously enlarged Prussian regimental barbarism, a purely military state.[2]

In due course Rudolf and Frederick William became close friends. Historical precedent had been an initial barrier, for the German crown prince's skill as a military leader had been largely responsible for the defeat of Austrian forces at Königgrätz. But gradually Rudolf, partly as a result of the prince of Wales's influence, came to see that he was no typical Prussian, and that they had much in common. It was chiefly the crown princess's admiration for Rudolf that persuaded Queen Victoria to moderate her views of him, for she had once regarded him as an incorrigible rake. She was so scandalised by reports of his private life that she had almost refused her eldest son permission to attend his wedding in 1881. Even the prince of Wales, after showing Rudolf around London in 1878, had remarked that it was surprising how much the young man knew about sexual matters; 'There is nothing I could teach him'.[3] One detects an unconscious note of envy.

There was no love lost between Rudolf and his close contemporary in age, Prince William of Germany. Rudolf thought him unbearably arrogant, personifying all that he found repellent in imperial Germany. In turn William regarded the former as irresponsible, a dangerous radical and atheist, and insufferably bookish. Despite their political differences, Bismarck admired Rudolf for his keen intellectual gifts, above all his exhaustive history of the Austro-Hungarian monarchy, which he began in 1884. With his abiding interest in history and modern scientific developments – highlighted in his speech on the opening of an electrical exhibition in Vienna in August 1883 – Rudolf closely resembled the prince consort. Had Albert still been alive, he would have found a kindred spirit in the young crown prince of Austria-Hungary.

One of Rudolf's closest friends in Austria was Moritz Szeps, editor of *Neues Wiener Tageblatt*. It was a friendship of which Francis Joseph strongly disapproved, thinking both Jews and journalists to be beneath consideration – and a Jewish journalist as certainly no company for his heir. Szeps and Rudolf, who took an instant liking to each other on their first meeting in 1881, used to meet secretly in a small apartment in the Hofburg. Long political discussions took place, and it was in this way that Rudolf learnt much of the world beyond the narrow horizons of Viennese court life.

Szeps had high hopes for the future:

> When Franz Joseph is gone, he will leave such a mess behind him that the worst is bound to happen! We shall get a revolution with bloodshed and a Separatist movement that will break up the Empire. And when I think of that splendid son of his! . . . In Rudolf we shall have an Emperor suited to modern needs. What a future for Europe to look forward to! With Frederick III on the German throne, and Rudolf on the Austro-Hungarian, the parties of reaction would receive their death-blow. A marvellous prospect dependent on one man![4]

In September 1885 the prince of Wales paid a second visit to Hungary, solely for the purpose of sport, and for much of the time he was accompanied by Rudolf. In the same way that Elizabeth found foxhunting in Ireland much better than that in England, so the prince discovered great enjoyment in shooting over the Hungarian countryside with its picturesque views and plentiful game reserves. At Udvarhely, as a guest of Count Festetics, he enjoyed the facilities which had made it such a spectacular hunting ground for medieval kings. The estate covered 40,000 acres, with stags not merely roaming the plains singly, as they did at Balmoral, but in wild herds. The prince and his suite rose at 4.30 every morning, returning for breakfast at 9.30, and then out in the late afternoon for another three hours at 4 p.m.

In October he stayed in Budapest for a few days with Count Karolyi. According to the strongly Anglophobe German minister Baron von Holstein, here he led such a fast life 'that even the Hungarians shook their heads'.

The three princes were present at two grand imperial celebrations during 1887. In March that year the prince of Wales and Crown Prince Rudolf were guests at Berlin for the ninetieth birthday festivities of Emperor William. At the time European affairs were overshadowed by a quarrel between Austria and Russia in the Balkans, complicated by Tsar Alexander III's conviction that England had completely withdrawn from European politics and was too ill-equipped to dare go to war.

Shortly after his arrival in Germany, Rudolf had a long conversation with the crown prince and princess. The latter reported to Queen Victoria that Rudolf, unlike them, believed war to be inevitable:

> He spoke of the intense desirability of a close understanding between England, and said that the Austrian government dreaded

not being able to secure some sort of useful understanding, as though Lord Salisbury might be willing, yet English cabinets changed so often, and with them the policy of the country, that it made it so difficult to rely on England's help and her word. He repeated that Count Kalnoky* was most English in his feelings and sympathies – that Sir A. Paget† had a most excellent position at Vienna and was very much liked there. . .(he) thinks that if Germany helps Austria against Russia, the French will instantly attack Germany and that the coming war will be extremely serious![5]

In a similar conversation with Bismarck, Rudolf was told that Germany wanted a firm alliance with Austria in the event of a war against France and Russia simultaneously. He wished to come to terms with England and Italy, and appeared to favour an Austro-Anglo-Italian alliance. Yet Rudolf had learnt from experience, and had been warned by the crown prince and princess, that Bismarck was not to be trusted. What he said and what he did were often very different.

In a letter home, Rudolf commented prophetically that the Emperor William was unlikely to survive much longer, as he looked so terrible and appeared very feeble. Ironically he attached no significance to the hoarseness in Crown Prince Frederick William's throat, as the latter delivered a speech congratulating his father on his birthday.

The threat of war had receded by June 1887, as a galaxy of monarchs, crown princes, archdukes and other royalty descended on London to celebrate Queen Victoria's jubilee. On the prince of Wales fell much of the burden of entertaining foreign and colonial visitors. Rudolf represented the Austro-Hungarian empire, and wrote enthusiastically to Stephanie of the endless whirl of activity, plus a special honour bestowed personally on him by the grandmama of Europe:

> I can send you no more than a few lines, for I am frightfully rushed, and I really have no time to spare. The old Queen came to-day, was most friendly, and bestowed on me the Order of the Garter, pinning it on herself, and fondling me as she did so, so that I could hardly refrain from laughing. As to your parents, I only saw them during the ceremony,‡ since no one has any free time . . .[6]

The prince of Wales told Rudolf's adjutant, Count Kinsky of the Austrian embassy, that 'he was very glad because it was a particular,

---

*Austrian minister of foreign affairs.
†British ambassador to Vienna.
‡The service of thanksgiving at Westminster Abbey.

quite exceptional distinction, as the order was usually only granted to members of the family or to reigning princes'.[7]

Rudolf had indeed made an excellent impression on the queen, and on everyone else. His charm and courtesy were much talked about, and it was noticed that at dinner she walked in on his arm, in front of several crowned heads. The prince of Wales went out of his way to entertain Rudolf. On the night of his arrival, they went out to the Marlborough Club and stayed until 4 a.m. Count Kinsky organised a luncheon for him at a club in Richmond, and a supper with distinguished guests including the duchess of Manchester. At about 2 a.m. the prince of Wales asked the orchestra to play *Can-Can* from Offenbach's *Orpheus in the Underworld*, and partnered the duchess in dancing with almost embarrassing fervour. Though Rudolf was no prude, he was moved to ask one of his fellow-guests to suggest that the waiters might leave, as they must not see their future sovereign making such a clown of himself.

On another occasion they went to see Buffalo Bill at a music hall. Both princes were so fascinated that they arrived half an hour late for luncheon with the queen, who nonetheless graciously forgave them. No wonder Rudolf was 'frightfully rushed.'

Kinsky's impressions of the crown prince were mixed. On one hand, he was particularly pleased to see in him the 'Austrian grace of manner,' and also how much he appeared to look up to the emperor and regard his dignified behaviour as an example. The latter Kinsky had not expected, assuming that the headstrong young man's motto was 'opposition for the sake of opposition'.

But there was a darker side. Kinsky noted that the crown prince had tense nerves. His restlessness, his yearning to spend each day from dawn to dusk in a perpetual round of pleasure, made people anxious. He was physically tired, though he would not admit it, and while staying at Brown's Hotel, he was afraid to go out of the building after dark unaccompanied.

Rudolf's nervous behaviour was not the only shadow that darkened the jubilee celebrations for him. There were two other unhappy omens, both of which were secretly commented on at the time.

Of all those who honoured Queen Victoria in the stately procession to Westminster Abbey on 21 June, nobody looked more magnificent than the German crown prince. Frederick William in his gleaming white Cuirassier uniform towered splendidly above those riding next to him. It was not generally known that he was unable to speak above a whisper, and that the doctors suspected his persistent throat trouble to be cancer of the larynx. The long-cherished ambition of himself and his wife to reign over Germany and help create the climate for a more liberal, democratic era in the empire was in jeopardy. Both his brother-in-law and Rudolf also eagerly awaited the day when he would succeed his elderly father as emperor, and they watched him in London that summer with grave anxiety.

In Vienna, people were less concerned with his illness – which was not yet common knowledge in Austria, except in medical circles – than with the fact that their not very popular crown princess had not accompanied her husband to London. It was believed that she had refused to go out of sheer obstinacy, although it had been Francis Joseph's wish that they should both represent him at the festivities. In view of the close blood relationship between Queen Victoria and Stephanie, it was only to be expected.

The truth was revealed some months later. In a private *tête-à-tête* with the emperor's close companion, actress Katherine Schratt, Stephanie tearfully showed her a cutting from an English newspaper stating that the fifteen-year-old Marie Vetsera, niece of the Baltazzi brothers who had been so distrusted by Marie Festetics, was coming to London during the jubilee in order to meet Rudolf. The article, she said, had been sent to her by Marie Larisch, a niece of Empress Elizabeth noted for her perpetual lies and love of making mischief. Marie Larisch had been very close to Rudolf in his bachelor days, and despite her lowly birth she had once entertained the possibility of marrying him herself. Because of this she hated Stephanie with a vengeance, and took malicious pleasure in inventing wicked stories about his behaviour to upset her.

Captain Middleton later threw a slightly different light on events. He explained that Marie Vetsera's motives for going to London were not quite so underhand. Shortly before the jubilee, she had gone to visit her sister who lived in England, even though she may have been using this as an excuse to be near Rudolf, whom she could therefore see more often and less conspicuously on foreign territory than she could in Austria. But Stephanie's parents, parents-in-law, Queen Victoria and of course Rudolf himself were united in their anger that she should draw attention to the rift in their marriage so ostentatiously. It was said that Rudolf met Marie's mother Baroness Vetsera in London, and she urged him to rid himself of Stephanie once and for all. Whether this is true or not, by the time he returned to Vienna it was recognised that his marriage was beyond salvation.

At the court of Berlin, there was another cause of concern for Rudolf. By Christmas 1887, Crown Prince Frederick William's state of health was precarious. Too ill to return to Germany immediately after the jubilee celebrations and a period of convalescence at Balmoral, he and the crown princess had rented a villa at San Remo on the Riviera, considered to be the best place for a man whose condition was regarded as almost hopeless. It was feared that he might not even outlive his father.

However, on 9 March 1888 Emperor William passed away, within a fortnight of what would have been his ninety-first birthday. The close of his long life had brought an unintentionally comic moment to the Viennese. Black-bordered newspapers announced his demise to the Austrian capital, to be followed quickly by the arrival of telegrams saying that he had taken food and drunk champagne during the night. Either the venerable monarch had performed a feat unparalleled since the Holy Resurrection, or somebody was not telling the truth. When he finally expired next day, said Rudolf, 'the genuine tidings of the death were received with indifference, or with the feeling, "thanks be, at last there will be an end of these stories, one way or the other"'.[8] People were more concerned with a great fire which broke out in the middle of Vienna instead.

Emperor William's funeral was delayed in order to give his dying voiceless son, now Emperor Frederick III, time to travel comfortably from the sunny Mediterranean climate to a bitterly cold and snowy Berlin. He was too ill to attend the ceremony outdoors, and much against his will he was persuaded to watch from his palace window instead.

Among foreign royalties present were the prince of Wales, who curtailed his silver wedding festivities to do so, and Rudolf. Both men were visibly depressed at seeing the slow death of a close and much-respected friend on whose survival so much had depended.

For the prince of Wales, there was the added anguish of being about to lose his favourite brother-in-law. For Rudolf, parallels between his life and that of the dying emperor were frightening. Frederick had been relegated to a life of inactivity, forced to watch Bismarck's personal antagonism of most of Europe and pursue a reactionary policy which spelt trouble for the years ahead until it was too late. Rudolf himself had likewise been excluded from playing any political role by his father, while the chief minister Count Taaffe was by his intransigence threatening the stability of the Austro-Hungarian empire. In addition, both heirs were repelled by the sight of Crown Prince William strutting around full of his own importance, doing nothing to dispel the impression that he could not wait to become emperor himself.

Queen Victoria set out on her travels for Florence in mid-March. From there she announced her intention of going to visit Emperor Frederick at Berlin. The plan was greeted with howls of protest, chiefly because it was suspected that she would lend her support to a proposal of marriage between her granddaughter Princess Victoria of Prussia and Alexander of Battenberg, formerly sovereign prince of Bulgaria. The idea of such a match had bitterly divided the family on personal and political grounds, foremost among the latter being that

Alexander was fiercely hated by Tsar Alexander III and that for Emperor Frederick and Queen Victoria to sanction the marriage would be to cause bad blood between Germany and Russia.

Nevertheless Queen Victoria refused to be deterred by Bismarck's threats of resignation, and contemptuously dismissed her prime minister Lord Salisbury's pleas that she should at least take a minister with her. It was not a political visit, she insisted, and in any case she had already advised her daughter Empress Victoria against pursuing the Battenberg match.

Francis Joseph eagerly seized the chance of m. ~ting Queen Victoria for the first time in twenty-five years. His motives were inspired partly by courtesy, natural good manners towards a fellow-sovereign travelling through his territory, and partly by a desire to further Anglo-Austrian harmony following the excellent impression Rudolf had made at the jubilee. The queen was displeased, for she did not wish to give Bismarck the suspicion that her journey was for anything other than family reasons. However, to decline Francis Joseph's invitation would be to commit the same breach of royal etiquette that Empress Elizabeth had habitually done in Britain.

On the afternoon of 23 April 1888, a hot fine day, the royal train pulled into Innsbruck. The emperor, in full uniform, had been travelling from Vienna for seventeen hours to receive the queen, her daughter Beatrice, and son-in-law Henry of Battenberg, and welcomed them as they were escorted on to the platform. They lunched *à quatre,* though Queen Victoria was exhausted by her journey and the heat:

> I unfortunately had a very bad sick headache and could eat next to nothing. The Emperor was most kind, and talked very pleasantly on many subjects. He said how happy he was at the good relations existing between our two countries, which he hoped would continue, as in case of war we could act together. Russia was incomprehensible, and he thought Bismarck much too weak and yielding to Russia, which was a great mistake. After a very affectionate leave-taking, we went on. . . [9]

Francis Joseph and Rudolf may have differed in their political outlook and indeed their sympathy for the liberal opinions of the ill-fated Emperor Frederick. But father and son were united in their apprehension of what would happen when he died. They considered that Crown Prince William's foreign policy, at one with the ideas of Bismarck, would be to favour Russia at Austria's expense. In addition, they found his 'posturing', swaggering behaviour acutely painful to watch. He made an embarrassing contrast to his kindly, dignified father.

Yet at least Francis Joseph was bound by reasons of respect for tradition to Germany as an ally, regardless of who ruled the German empire, while Rudolf was emphatically not. Some forty years later, as an exile in the Netherlands, ex-Emperor William II commented in his memoirs sardonically that the Austrian crown prince's 'soul revolted from the Prussian idea.'[10]

On 15 June 1888 the sorely-tried Emperor Frederick breathed his last. With him perished the hopes of his wife, his brother-in-law in England, Crown Prince Rudolf in particular, and of liberals throughout Europe and Germany in general. Rudolf was on a visit to the provinces of Bosnia and Herzegovina when he received news of his close friend's death, and he and the prince of Wales attended the funeral at Berlin. The sad ceremony was overshadowed by allegations that the prince of Wales asked in private conversation whether it was true that the late emperor had intended to cede Alsace and Lorraine, French territories handed over to Germany after the Franco-Prussian war, back to France.

Personal antagonism between the future King Edward VII and Emperor William II, which was to colour Anglo-European relations vividly until the former's death in 1910, was marked in the autumn of 1888 by what became known as the 'Vienna incident'. Not only were uncle and nephew at the centre of this personal quarrel, but the Austrian emperor and crown prince were also involved.

During the summer, Francis Joseph invited the prince of Wales to attend autumn military manoeuvres of the Austrian army, in his capacity as honorary colonel of the Austrian 12th Hussars. The prince understood that Emperor William would be paying an official visit to Vienna at about the same time, and wrote two friendly letters expressing pleasure at the likelihood of their meeting on that occasion. To his dismay, neither was acknowledged. Yet he went to Vienna as planned, arriving at the Grand Hotel on 10 September in time for breakfast.

After his meal, he donned his colonel's red and gold uniform, and prepared to receive the Austrian emperor and crown prince. They asked how he would like to be entertained, and accordingly drew up a programme which involved his absence from Vienna on 3 October. After he had approved it in principle. he was told casually by the emperor that William II was due in the city on that date. The prince of Wales said immediately that he would return to Vienna on that day, and stay throughout his nephew's visit. His hosts left without comment, and after paying several calls, he dined that evening with Francis Joseph.

On the next day, the prince paid further calls in the city, and returned to the hotel to entertain Sir Augustus Paget and his wife to luncheon. Paget, however, arrived early and asked to see the prince's senior equerry, Major-General Arthur Ellis, alone and at once, with 'a most disagreeable communication'. The foreign minister Count Kalnoky had explained to Paget, not without embarrassment, that the German emperor had stipulated that no royal guests except himself should be in Vienna during his forthcoming visit.

The prince of Wales was genuinely astonished and hurt. He told Paget that he had wished to avoid provoking ill-natured gossip by staying away from the capital while his nephew was present. Nevertheless, within twenty-four hours it was common gossip throughout Vienna that Emperor William had threatened to cancel his visit unless the heir to the British throne was asked firmly to depart.

Bewildered, the prince of Wales discussed this turn of events with Rudolf. The latter told him bitterly that German agents had spread rumours that the prince wanted to interfere with forthcoming conversations between Francis Joseph and William II, and to embroil both with Tsar Alexander, so as to make mischief which could only be to the benefit of France and England. His presence in Vienna was therefore not required. Kalnoky had no intention of displeasing Austria's most powerful personal ally, albeit an unstable one, and decided that the private family quarrels of uncle and nephew would have to take place outside the Austro-Hungarian empire.

The prince of Wales had no alternative but to agree to go to Bucharest at the beginning of October, and stay with the king and queen of Roumania. Meanwhile he had to be entertained in Vienna, no easy task. Royalties throughout Europe were all too well aware of his boundless energy, his abhorrence of going to bed before the small hours, and his ill-concealed boredom if kept inactive. The problem was particularly acute in Vienna, for Hofburg family dinners were over by 10 p.m. Francis Joseph was always at his desk by 5 a.m. the next day, and unaccustomed to late nights.

Both princes applied themselves with gusto to the art of pleasure – hunting by day, receptions and parties by night. Even Rudolf, whose declining health was apparent to very few, was astonished at his friend's stamina. 'Wales,' he wrote to Stephanie (12 September), was 'in great fettle, wants to see everything and will not allow himself to be left out in the cold. Nothing seems to tire the old boy. I long for a rest.'[11]

At the same time he announced his intention of inviting 'Wales' to a bear shoot in October after his return from Roumania. Inspired perhaps by his knowledge of English history and the fate which had overtaken King William II in the New Forest several centuries earlier, he added that he would only invite the other William II 'in order to arrange a neat hunting accident which would remove him from the world'.[12]

While in Vienna the prince and Rudolf showed their contempt for public opinion by lunching openly in a restaurant with their old friend Baron Hirsch, a Jewish financier and philanthropist. Hirsch's personal fortune had been of considerable benefit to industry in the Austro-Hungarian empire, through his investment in railways and shipping lines in the Eastern Mediterranean, which might otherwise have had to close down through lack of capital. He had also lent money to Rudolf, whose personal income was slight in comparison with other crown princes of the time, and assisted Szeps in his financial difficulties with *Tagblatt*.

Less entertaining for the prince of Wales, but vital for the sake of diplomatic relations, was his attendance at military manoeuvres at Belovár. With his figure and chronic breathlessness, he was not one of nature's born horsemen, but the occasion demanded several arduous hours in the saddle that day. Francis Joseph was appreciative of the efforts his portly guest in Hungarian uniform was making, and reported to Katherine Schratt, showing a sense of humour which was rarely apparent:

> I tried my best to shake the Prince of Wales off with sustained spells at the trot or the gallop but I couldn't manage it; the plump fellow kept up the whole time and lasted out incredibly. But he did get pretty stiff, and as he had split his red Hussar trousers and had nothing on underneath, it was all rather unpleasant for him.[13]

After the closing manoeuvre, the emperor introduced the prince to General Hennenberg, Hungarian cavalry commander. The British heir congratulated him on the superb horsemanship of his hussars. He was astonished to be told that they were newly-formed army contingents made up of ordinary recruits.

Following a few days with the Roumanian royal couple at Sinaia in the first week of October, the prince joined Rudolf for more sport in Transylvania. The hills around Görgény-Szentimre were famous for their bear hunts, and when the Hungarian government learnt that their crown prince was a devotee of the sport, they presented him with the castle belonging to the fortress town, and shooting rights for miles around.

Unfortunately the bears proved as obstinate as the German emperor. After the hot dry summer, they had moved up into the mountains for shelter. Only three were seen the whole time, and they all escaped. Both princes and the other royal guests, the Austrian archdukes Frederick and Otto, and the duke of Braganza, were very disappointed. According to the prince of Wales, in a letter to his son George (12 October), Rudolf was 'dreadfully put out. . . but we were a very cheery party – capital cook, Hungarian band, and splendid weather'.[14] There were early morning rides up into the mountains, which started in four-in-hand horse carriages, transferring to pony-carts as paths became rougher. In the evening they enjoyed peasant dances by torchlight in the castle courtyard. Though good weather may have ruined hunting, the warm temperature brought blossom out on the pear trees in Görgény park for a second time that autumn.

From Görgény the princes went to Budapest for a couple of days. On 14 October they returned to Vienna, where attractions included 'a wonderfully good amateur Photographic Exhibition' and dinner at the Hofburg in honour of the prince of Wales and King Milan of Serbia, who met for the first time. That evening they attended the opening of the new Burgtheater; 'it was a great success and the house looked lovely'.[15]

Next morning they breakfasted early and went chamois-shooting in Styria, a hunt which the prince of Wales described incongruously as 'difficult – but the prettiest sport I have seen for a long time'.[16] It was a happy conclusion to his five weeks in central Europe, and he was in high spirits as he and Rudolf waved *Au revoir* – an ironic farewell – on the railway platform at Vienna.

Despite the social consolations, these few weeks left a sour taste in the mouths of many involved. Queen Victoria knew her eldest son's faults only too well, but she stood loyally by him against the grandson for whom she had so often gone out of her way to make allowances. She told Lord Salisbury that the German Emperor William's complaint that the prince of Wales had treated him as a nephew and not as an emperor was 'really too *vulgar* and too absurd, as well as untrue, almost *to be believed*. . . if he has *such* notions, he had better *never* come here'.[17] To the widowed Empress Frederick, who had been persecuted and reviled to a degree in the Prussian court (to no little extent by her own son) which horrified the family, the prince wrote sadly (31 October) that he must cease any further acquaintance with William 'till he makes some apology for the gross insult he has heaped upon me in a foreign country'.[18]

In his anger the prince of Wales was less tactful than usual. His comment that 'William the Great needs to learn that he is living at the end of the nineteenth century and not in the Middle Ages' was overheard and frequently repeated.

Francis Joseph had long since reached the time of life when petty personal differences could be disregarded, and he was less affected than anybody else by his fellow-emperor's behaviour. What irritated him was the fact that William's first visit abroad since his accession had been to Russia. Remembering Russian interference in the Balkans and her recent designs on Bulgaria, he viewed this as ominous. He instructed Taaffe to cancel a torchlight procession which German nationalists had arranged in Vienna to celebrate the German emperor's arrival, and warned him to keep an eye on William so that he should not be left alone in the city. In other words, he should have no opportunity to make mischief.

The Viennese made their lack of enthusiasm for their guest obvious, and William responded with typical displays of tactlessness which did nothing to change their minds. He bestowed the Order of the Black Eagle on Count Tisza, minister-president of Hungary, but pointedly excluded Taaffe from a similar honour.

The most damaging blow of all came soon after William had returned to Germany. He sent Francis Joseph a letter, drafted by Bismarck, demanding for the sake of Austro-German relations that the crown prince of Austria-Hungary be dismissed from the post of inspector-general of infantry, to which he had recently been appointed. Instead of treating this insolent message with the contempt it richly deserved, Francis Joseph invited his son for an official interview. He told him of the German emperor's complaints and criticisms, and asked if he was willing to resign of his own accord in the interests of the two empires' alliance.

Not surprisingly, Rudolf was bitterly angry and demoralised. He refused to consider resignation, and insisted that he was carrying out his duties conscientiously, working on a report on how to improve the army drill programme.

Some months later, the prince of Wales told Queen Victoria that this scene 'led directly to the catastrophe'.

For Rudolf, the year 1888 had opened badly. In January, he joined his father on a hunt, and narrowly avoided shooting him by mistake. It was only the prompt action of a beater, who raised his arm to protect the emperor and had his forearm shattered in the process, which prevented a fatal accident that could easily have been interpreted as something far more sinister. The death of Frederick III in June and subsequent accession of William II realised his worst fears, and the humiliating letter to Francis Joseph indicated only the first round in what promised to be an indefinite personal feud.

By October, Rudolf's entourage was becoming seriously alarmed about him. He seemed absent-minded at military parades and other public ceremonies, and frequently late in arriving. His interest in serious books had gone, and now he only read third-rate fiction of the variety he had once despised. Newspapers no longer held his attention, unless they contained reports of suicides and suicide pacts.* People commented on how grey and unwell he looked. Within the

---

* Of these was no shortage. Walburga, Lady Paget, reported that Vienna was notorious for her epidemic of suicides at the end of the nineteenth century. She was warned not to ride in the Prater early each morning before patrols had taken corpses off the trees.

previous two years he had suffered successively from gonorrhoea, bronchitis, inflammation of the eyes (he feared himself to be in danger of going blind), and a severe fall from his horse. Morphine had been prescribed for him, and in an age when less was known about drug addiction, he had become heavily dependent.

Although his marriage to Stephanie had collapsed in all but name, she was the one person sufficiently appalled by his deteriorating condition to try and help him. His father did not or would not recognise the danger signs, and in any case had avoided more contact with him than necessary since the shooting accident in January. His mother was cruising round the Greek islands, too full of the poetry of Heine and Byron to trouble herself with tiresome considerations like her family. One day Stephanie took her courage in both hands. Though it was contrary to Habsburg etiquette to approach His Imperial Majesty without an appointment, she asked the chamberlain to announce her into the study. She had hardly begun to explain Rudolf's case and put forward her proposal that he be given a complete rest and sent abroad on indefinite leave before Francis Joseph interrupted her, saying that she was giving way to fantasies and there was nothing wrong with his son apart from a tendency to expect too much of himself. In future, he intimated firmly, she should only approach him through an equerry. With that another door was closed – in more senses than one.

The last few weeks of Rudolf's life, his association with the helplessly-infatuated seventeen-year-old Marie Vetsera, and events which led to the discovery of their dead bodies at the Mayerling hunting lodge on 30 January 1889, have inspired countless theories, books of widely differing value, films, plays and even ballets. No royal death since the mystery of King Edward IV of England's eldest sons, the 'princes in the tower', has been so hotly debated. Nothing would be gained by examining the endless speculation at length here. Suffice it to say that the popular explanation, that Rudolf shot Marie and then turned the revolver on himself, is the most probable.

The public were informed in a special edition of *Wiener Zeitung* that their crown prince had died of apoplexy. Next day, it was announced that this initial report was incorrect. His imperial highness had appeared to be suffering from some form of nervous disturbance during the last few weeks of his life, and he had killed himself in a moment of mental derangement. No mention, naturally, was made of the fact that he had not been alone that night at Mayerling. But the Viennese realised that there was something extremely suspicious about his death. It must have been obvious to those who discovered his body that he did not die of natural causes. Why was this not revealed to them with the first news of his passing? As *The Times* told its readers in London, the official statement of the facts was the only one which found no general acceptance.

At home, Francis Joseph was bowed down by grief and shame. He had lost his only son, and more importantly his heir, in circumstances almost too dreadful to contemplate. After rising to the occasion as she could do in moments of extreme crisis, Elizabeth sank back into her private world of melancholy. From this time onwards she nearly always wore black, and hid her face behind a fan on the rare instances that she ventured outside her own intimate circle.

In England, the prince of Wales was horrified at the fate that had befallen his friend. He had met Marie Vetsera at a race meeting in Germany, and like many other men had found her pretty and charming. Ironically he pointed her out to Rudolf when they attended the opening of the new Burgtheater in October 1888, and noticed that he appeared to take no interest in her at the time. Perhaps Albert Edward felt guilt at not having seen the decline in his health on their last hunting expeditions, not realising that he was 'dreadfully put out' by circumstances other than the failure of their bear hunt in Transylvania. He had known about Rudolf's moods of intense depression, but never thought that it could end in such tragedy.

Though she had strongly disapproved of his private life, and now forbade the prince of Wales to attend the funeral at Vienna, Queen Victoria could never forget how Rudolf had charmed her at the jubilee in 1887. 'Terribly upset,' she ciphered to Sir Augustus Paget on 1 February for 'all details you can gather however distressing they may be'. There was more to this than idle curiosity, for as she told Prince Philip of Coburg, she wished to be able to contradict wild rumours. To Lord Salisbury, she wrote that

> The Prince of Wales has seen a friend of his from Vienna, who is a great personal friend of the Emperor, and he knows all the details, which he gave to the Prince of Wales, and which he says are too shocking to write. But there is no doubt that the poor Crown Prince was quite *off his head*.[19]

The prime minister apparently believed that Rudolf did not take his own life. Already it was whispered that somebody else had pulled the trigger, and his death had been a carefully-contrived assassination. There was no shortage of suspects or motives. A cuckolded forester had sought revenge; French or Hungarian patriots had killed him because they felt betrayed by his refusal to do more for their countries than they believed he had promised; agents of Count Taaffe or an execution squad under orders from the emperor's elderly cousin Archduke Albrecht, inspector general of the army, had exacted the ultimate penalty because he was too deeply involved in treason against the state, knowing that he was a potential suicide and therefore safe in the knowledge that nobody would suspect he had been judicially eliminated.

None of these arguments was believed by the prince of Wales. He wrote to Queen Victoria (12 February) that

> . . .you tell me that Lord Salisbury is positive that poor Rudolf and that unfortunate young lady were murdered – all I can say is that everything points to suicide – I have seen an Austrian gentleman who has just come from Vienna – and who is a personal friend of the Emperor and Empress and knew poor Rudolf since his childhood who in the long conversation I had with him entirely corroborated all Sir A. Paget wrote to you – even giving more sad details – It seems poor Rudolf has had suicide on the brain for some time past – he wrote letters saying he was going to die – and the poor young lady wrote the same to her family – He shot her first – then decked her out with flowers – and then blew his brains out – and he had only half an hour for all this – He wrote to his Mother, wife, youngest sister, two cousins and some personal friends but not to his Father and I am assured that some of his letters were quite incoherent – Nobody knew that the young lady was with him but his valet. The latter seems to have had orders from the Emperor not to leave him alone – but he peremptorily ordered him away – against the poor Man's wishes before the deed was done – My friend told me that there was some unknown reason why he committed suicide and he does not believe that it was on account of the young lady. It has been ascertained that on January 13th, he seduced her and committed the last fatal act on 30th! There are details I could tell you – which I cannot write – which clearly shew complete aberration of the mind for some time past – the whole story is like a bad dream and I can think of nothing else. . .[20]

Had Rudolf not died at Mayerling, it was unlikely that he would have lived much longer, such was his physical and mental state. The emperor's apparently speedy recovery from grief at his bereavement was attributed to results of an autopsy, revealing symptoms of advanced paralysis which would have probably led to the crown prince's demise from natural causes within twelve months. Even if he had survived his father and ascended the imperial throne, he would have perhaps been mentally incapable of discharging the duties of an emperor with any great success.

Moreover, like his close friend Emperor Frederick III, it is tempting to wonder whether he possessed the stamina to surmount the difficulties which faced them in their hopes of introducing constitutional rule into countries which were still ruled almost as autocratically as they had been in the revolutionary year of 1848. Had they been put to the test, they would have chosen their ministers and advisers wisely, and in so doing would have striven to create a healthy political climate in which progressive ideas could flourish.

But forces of counter-reaction, as personified in Austria by Taaffe and in Germany by Bismarck, were again dominant. In the 1870s liberalism had been in the ascendant throughout both empires, being essential to economic progress, but within a decade it had served its purpose to many. Liberals were hounded by the reactionaries, seeing in them the threat of political progress which ran directly against state interests and the powers of the few.

Captain Middleton coldly dismissed the memory of Rudolf, remarking bluntly that the most interesting thing about him had been his death. To him it appeared impossible that the crown prince would have taken his own life, as it required moral courage to commit suicide. However, Middleton's judgement can hardly be regarded as objective. He had clearly never forgiven Rudolf for turning his back on him at their first – and probably only – meeting in London in 1878.

Perhaps the last word on Rudolf should go to Queen Victoria, who commented with heartfelt sympathy in a letter to Lord Salisbury (3 February) that he was 'singularly gifted and accomplished, and with large liberal views & was looked upon as one likely to withstand the 2 Bismarcks' tyranny and dangerous views'.[21]

The second part of this verdict was a trifle optimistic, but in it she recognised the hopes which had once rested on him. In happier circumstances, this talented prince might have brought the Habsburg monarchy into the twentieth century in more ways than one, just as Frederick III might have done for the Hohenzollerns.

CHAPTER 6

Twilight of a century

The shots which rang out at Queretaro in June 1867 had ended one phase in the relationship between British and Austrian royalty. The bullets at Mayerling some two decades later closed another door. For the last twelve years of Queen Victoria's reign, contacts were few and far between. The prince of Wales's hopes that a more modern-thinking monarch would soon reign over the Austro-Hungarian empire had been dashed, and Austria was no longer so diplomatically important to him. This would be the case until his own accession to the throne.

Such visits as the British heir paid to the empire over the next few years were of a merely social nature. In October 1890 he and a large party of friends including Lady Randolph Churchill, Lady Lilian Wemyss, and Lord and Lady Georgiana Curzon, reached Vienna. After laying a wreath on Rudolf's tomb, he gave a luncheon party for Hirsch and King George of Greece at the Grand Hotel. Next they left by train for St Johann, near Hohenau on the Austro-Hungarian border. The following ten days saw an orgy of shooting, with an estimated 20,000 partridges shot. The prince wrote to Prince George (19 October) that 'this certainly beats everything on record and will quite spoil me for any shooting at home'.[1] All birds flew high and well because Hirsch, who employed several hundred beaters, had devoted an unprecedented degree of technical skill to the organisation of that massacre. The 'unpretentious' house he found 'most comfortable'.

Exhilarated and refreshed by his activities, the prince returned to Vienna, where he called informally on all resident archdukes and dined with the emperor, who accompanied him to the opera.

During the unhappy summer of 1891, when the prince of Wales was harassed by the twin scandals of the Tranby Croft baccarat case and the Beresford affair, he sought refuge again in the Austro-Hungarian empire. In Vienna there was criticism of such unseemly behaviour from a colonel-proprietor of an Austrian regiment, and officers in the imperial army were as censorious as those in England

of His Royal Highness's conception of military duty and example. To
them it was

> simply unimaginable that a German, Austrian or French Field-
> Marshal should sit down to win money from or lose money to a
> mere lieutenant, who, if he gambles, must be paying away his
> father's money or prematurely squandering his inheritance.[2]

It was therefore to Hungary that Prince Albert Edward departed,
staying with Baron Hirsch for another few weeks of shooting. In one
week, it was reported that they killed 11,000 partridges.

During the first fifty-eight years of her reign, Queen Victoria had met
Emperor Francis Joseph only twice, and almost quarter of a century
separated each occasion. As she approached her sixtieth year on the
throne, both sovereigns were to meet twice within the space of a year.

For three successive winters Empress Elizabeth stayed at Cap
Martin in the south of France. Over the years she had become more
obsessed than ever about her figure, and punished herself with endless
'cures' so immoderately that she regularly suffered from digestive
disorders. By now she was taking little nourishment apart from milk,
and as it had to be as pure as possible, a special herd of cows was
bought and maintained for the purpose.

When he felt he could leave Austria for a few days at a time, the
emperor would come south to keep her company and try to persuade
her to follow a more normal diet. For him to take a holiday himself
was out of the question, as even when he stayed at Cap Martin he had
drafted about fifty telegrams and read a pile of despatches by 6 a.m.
each day when his adjutant came on duty.

In March 1896 it was rumoured that Queen Victoria was also about
to take a winter holiday on the Riviera, and would stay at the Grand
Hotel de Cimiez. To Valerie, the empress wrote that the queen had
taken the whole hotel and two villas, as she was bringing about
seventy people, among them her Indian servants; 'It must be a great
pleasure to travel like a circus.'[3] There was more unconscious envy
than sour cynicism in her words, for Elizabeth was fascinated by these
oriental servants in their exotic costumes. Even now the colourful and
unconventional still held an aura of excitement for her.

Queen, emperor and empress met on 13 March. The queen noted in
her journal that the empress was

> much altered and has lost all her beauty, except her figure, which
> remains the same. The Emperor was very kind. . .and I asked
> him to accept the Colonelcy in Chief of the King's 1st Dragoon
> Guards, which seemed to please him very much. The Empress

left sooner, saying she thought I might like to speak to the Emperor. He expressed the hope that our two countries would be on the best of terms – understood that we could not bind ourselves to any particular action beforehand, though I think he regretted it, but I tried to reassure him. He regretted the state of Turkey, – William's* imprudence, but trusted England and Germany would always keep well together.[4]

This meeting was evidently a sad one. Perhaps Queen Victoria noticed what their daughter Valerie had already perceived in the miserable weeks after Mayerling. Emperor and empress had drifted so far apart temperamentally by now that they had hardly anything in common except for their grief.

A year later, the two sovereigns met again at Cimiez. Queen Victoria noted in her journal (17 March 1897) that the emperor called on her after luncheon:

> He was most kind and amiable. I asked him to call me "Du", which seemed to please him. He is distressed at the Cretan troubles, but rejoices greatly at the union of the Great Powers, and thinks there can be no general war.[5]

The prospect of a 'general war' had arisen over a dispute between Greece and the island of Crete, which was part of the Turkish empire but largely Greek in population. After riots and virtual civil war on the island, the Greek government sent troops to help protect the Greek inhabitants, who clamoured for union with their mother country. Greece and Turkey prepared for war, until Lord Salisbury proposed a compromise on behalf of the powers. This was that, while Crete could not be annexed to Greece, self-government free of the Turkish yoke should be established, and pending this Greek troops were to leave the island forthwith. Turkey accepted this solution, but Greece refused to remove her army of occupation. As a result war was declared in April, and Turkey emerged victorious. By the following month, Greece was compelled to accept Cretan autonomy and remove her forces from Crete, and in addition had to pay the Turks a heavy indemnity.

Francis Joseph may have been pleased at the union of the powers, but not all the imperial family shared his feelings. After Rudolf's death, the emperor's heir was technically his thrice-married brother Charles Ludwig, whose intense Christian faith bordered on religious mania. His apparent simple-mindedness, ineptitude and indifferent health

---

* The German emperor.

made him unsatisfactory in the eyes of the empire for grooming as next head of state. He was therefore passed over in favour of his eldest son Francis Ferdinand, a fortuitous move in view of Charles Ludwig's death in May 1896. His religious fervour had proved his undoing. On a pilgrimage to the Holy Land he drank from the sacred but notoriously infested waters of the river Jordan, and died of typhoid within a few days.

Francis Ferdinand was intelligent but obstinate, and reputed to be one of the most politically-prejudiced men in the empire. His resentment of Hungarian aspirations, in particular, was matched by few if any of his uncle's ministers. Outside affairs of state it was maintained that his chief interests were hunting, to a degree which bordered on wholesale slaughter, and collecting statuettes of St Hubertus, patron saint of hunters. Paradoxically there was a gentler side to his involvement with natural history. He had a passion for flowers, and also collected both pressed plants and books on the subject until he knew the scientific names for all species and varieties as well as any botanical expert.

His hunting activities were curtailed from time to time by tuberculosis, the disease which had killed his mother, born Princess Maria Annunciata of Naples, at the age of twenty-eight. Doubts were sometimes entertained as to whether he would outlive the nineteenth century, let alone survive Francis Joseph. For several years he moved from sanatorium to sanatorium in warmer climates, in order to effect a recovery.

From his sickbed at Cannes, he regarded the pro-English policy of Count Goluchowski, minister of the exterior, as a betrayal of Austrian interests. To Prince Francis Liechtenstein, Austrian ambassador at St Petersburg, he wrote (14 November 1897):

> This fraternization with England which he has staged I consider exceedingly dangerous, or, to call it by its right name, nonsensical, because England is the most calculating, deceitful and unreliable ally on earth. I believe that there is no longer a sensible, thinking man who does not know that the Armenian horrors and the affair at Crete were directly inspired by England. By this close association with English ideas he estranges us entirely from Germany which has just now spoken very plainly and creates discord with Russia.[6]

The archduke's attitude to Great Britain, like that of the German emperor, was a mixture of admiration and jealousy. He was impressed by British world supremacy and the effortless ease with which she apparently administered her empire. According to Francis Joseph's adjutant Count Margutti,

> His sympathies with Great Britain were deep and genuine. He was impressed by English life and habits and in many respects the Anglo-Saxons, with their positivism, energy and respect for law and

order, had natural affinities with the serious and self-contained character of the Archduke.[7]

Above all, as an admiral and influential patron of the Austrian navy, he respected Britain's mighty fleet and maritime powers. At the same time, he was repelled by what he termed British arrogance. Of this he had had first-hand experience, in the course of a cruise around the Indian coast, undertaken largely for reasons of health. At an official banquet in Bombay in January 1893 given in his honour, he had been taken aback by the customs of the Victorian Raj, which decreed that the health of Queen-Empress Victoria was proposed first – before the toast to the guest's sovereign, as was the continental custom. This indignation at British superiority, and the manner in which she took her exalted status for granted, had been reinforced by events while he was in Egypt a couple of years later, when the British were despatching an army to the Sudan in order to put down an insurrection led by the Mahdi. Britain's policy, he fulminated, was one of 'lies and deception'.

Despite this, there was talk of an English princess being offered as the future bride of Archduke Francis Ferdinand, though it is unsubstantiated by any surviving letters in British or Austrian archives. In his biography of Francis Joseph, Baron Margutti alleged that he saw a letter from Sandringham, sent to the archduke sometime during the 1890s. Discreetly he asked whether His Imperial Highness cherished hopes of a union with Queen Victoria's granddaughter, and was given an evasive answer to the effect that such a marriage was 'a matter of such uncertainty' that it was 'better not to think about it'. The princess in question was 'Princess Mary [sic], the eldest daughter of the then Prince of Wales'.[8] By a process of elimination this was probably the second daughter Victoria, who remained 'poor Toria', an embittered spinster to the end of her days in December 1935.*

In 1897 England staged what was to be her last great celebration of the century, Queen Victoria's diamond jubilee. The chief event of this was a procession through London from Buckingham Palace to St Paul's Cathedral for the service of thanksgiving on 22 June, 'a never-to-be-forgotten day' as she called it in her journal. 'No-one ever, I believe, has met with such an ovation as was given to me'.[9] It was more of a festival of colonial and imperial splendour than a gathering of crowned heads and their representatives from Europe, though the Habsburgs were represented by Francis Ferdinand, who

* Her full names were Victoria Alexandra Mary. Her sisters, Louise and Maud, were married in 1889 and 1896 respectively; neither bore the name Mary.

stayed at Buckingham Gate with a small suite including his physician (and later biographer) Dr Victor Eisenmenger. He took part in the procession, cutting a dignified figure on horseback in his Hussar's uniform. That evening he attended dinner at the palace, seated between the queen herself and the Empress Frederick. What Her Majesty thought of him is not known, though close observers commented afterwards that she was impatient of his inability to speak English. Nonetheless there was no time for the family to pass judgment, however fleeting, on their guests. As the Empress Frederick reported to her daughter Sophie, crown princess of the Hellenes, Buckingham Palace was 'like a beehive, the place is so crammed we do not see so very much of each other'.[10]

It might be supposed that Queen Victoria looked on the archduke less than warmly because of memories of 1889. Ten years before, she had been captivated by the then Habsburg emissary, Crown Prince Rudolf. In view of the fate that befell him soon afterwards, any member of the Austrian reigning house from Rudolf's generation was a reminder of those grim events at Mayerling which she would rather have forgotten. What impression Francis Ferdinand made, if any, on the prince of Wales must likewise be guessed at, but the latter must also have felt a twinge of sadness as he reflected on how the last Austro-Hungarian heir had enjoyed himself at the previous jubilee. Certainly the archduke's morose manner did not endear him to those who were meeting him for the first time and remembered all too well Rudolf's easy-going demeanour.

Eisenmenger, if not his master as well, had nothing but praise for what he called respectfully 'the giant festival', and England's unstinting efforts to succeed in impressing her foreign visitors; 'Everybody knew his place, no excitement, no trouble, no accident but thorough efficiency everywhere.'[11]

In 1898 the citizens of Austria celebrated the golden jubilee of Emperor Francis Joseph's reign. But their empress was in no condition to take any part. Years of injudicious dieting and excessive exercise, a rash brought on by nervous eczema, and chronic insomnia, had all conspired to turn Elizabeth into a virtual invalid by the age of sixty. Her habitual depression had been exacerbated by the tragic death of her sister Sophie, duchess of Alençon, burnt to death in a fire at a charity bazaar in Paris the previous summer.

Elizabeth spent the spring of 1898 at Kissingen. Francis Joseph joined her briefly, and though he was prepared to find her looking tired and unwell he was shocked at her sluggish gait. She had always been an indefatigable walker, but now it was an effort for her to drag herself around on foot. Husband and wife spent a few days of summer together at Ischl. On 3 July an official bulletin announced that, while the empress's health gave no cause for anxiety, it was necessary for her to go for treatment at Bad Nauheim. On 16 July she left for what she described as 'this tiresome cure', each having a premonition that they might never see each other again.

From Nauheim she wrote affectionately, begging him to join her in Switzerland shortly. With a heavy heart, he replied that it was impossible for him to get away because of the autumn manoeuvres and jubilee festivities. Nonetheless, when she arrived at Caux in late August, she was in better health and spirits than she had been for a long time.

On 8 September the emperor wrote cheerfully to Katherine Schratt that at last he had really good news from the empress. She was taking walks without over-exerting herself and planning further expeditions.

Two days later, Elizabeth and her lady-in-waiting Countess Sztaray were shopping in Geneva. As they walked along the quay towards their boat for Territet, a man suddenly bumped into them, raising his fist against the empress and knocking her over. Insisting that she was more frightened than hurt, she was quickly helped to her feet. As she and the countess walked on board, she suddenly turned very pale and collapsed. All attempts to revive her proved futile. A nurse ordered attendants to loosen her clothing, and a small stab wound from a steel file was discovered on her left breast. She died without regaining consciousness.*

At Schönbrunn, Francis Joseph was in the study writing to his wife. As his adjutant Count Paar requested an urgent audience, he realised that something was terribly wrong. Paar, in great agitation, brought with him a telegram from Geneva to say that the empress was seriously injured. Minutes later, an aide-de-camp came with a second telegram announcing that Her Majesty had just passed away.

Queretaro. . .Mayerling. . .Geneva. Another name in the gazetteer of violent death *en famille* for the lonely emperor.

Among messages of condolence to the grief-stricken widower was a telegram from Queen Victoria at Balmoral, shocked by the assassination:

> Words fail me to express to Your Majesty my warm sympathy and my horror. It is too terrible, too cruel. May God protect and support you.[12]

From Schönbrunn he wired the following day:

> Deeply moved by the words of sincerest sympathy in my pain that is unutterable, I ask you to accept my warmest thanks for your kind condolence.[13]

---

* The assassin was a young Italian vagrant with anarchist sympathies, named Luigi Luccheni. Proud of his crime, he made no effort to resist arrest, and was sentenced to life imprisonment. In October 1910 he hanged himself in his cell.

Elizabeth's body was brought back to Vienna on 15 September and lay in state for two days before she found her last resting place in the Habsburg family vaults. After the funeral, the emperor wrote what was to be his last letter to Queen Victoria:

> After that difficult hour in which I accompanied my deeply loved wife on her last journey, the only thing that can give me comfort is so affectionate a remembrance as I have just received from you. I thank you with all my heart for including in your prayers her who is unforgettable, and myself also. I pray fervently to God that he may give you his full blessing.[14]

Among wreaths at the funeral was one from Queen Victoria of pale pink chrysanthemums, violets, lilies and palm leaves, inscribed 'A token of the deepest friendship and veneration from her faithful sister', and one from the prince and princess of Wales consisting of roses, violets and silver palms, accompanied by a white satin ribbon bearing the verse:

> Sister, thou art gone before us,
> And thy saintly soul is flown
> Where tears are wiped from every eye,
> And sorrow is unknown.[15]

Among other royalties, Elizabeth had no more devoted or understanding friend than the Empress Frederick, who respected her independence of mind. To Queen Victoria, she wrote (12 September) that, while the Austrian empress was so melancholy and unhappy it must have been a blessing for her to be at rest, 'the terrible way of being hurried to one's grave, struck down by the dagger of an assassin, a helpless, harmless woman, a guest in a strange country, is too dreadful for words!'[16]

In England, nobody had cherished the memory of Elizabeth more deeply than Captain Middleton. Whenever he spoke of the empress after her hunting expeditions in the British Isles had ceased, Margutti recorded after meeting him in the south of France, 'his usually dry and anything but fluent conversation at once became animated and phrases almost poetical crept in'.[17] It was the captain's opinion that a prolonged holiday in the English shires would have assuaged her grief after Rudolf's death more effectively than her aimless wanderings throughout Europe. 'What a pity she didn't come to us in England! We'd soon have got her back to life!'*

---

* Margutti does not date this conversation. He gives the impression that it took place sometime after the empress's assassination, though in fact Middleton was killed in a hunting accident in 1892, six years previously.

CHAPTER 7

'The most influential man of the present day'

'Another year begun,' Queen Victoria recorded in her journal on 1 January 1901, 'and I am feeling so weak and unwell that I enter upon it sadly.'[1] Increasing fatigue, indigestion, failing eyesight, and anxiety over British reverses in the Boer war had weakened her resistance to bad family news. During the previous summer she learned that the Empress Frederick was slowly dying of cancer, the disease which had claimed the life of the emperor and more recently that of the duke of Edinburgh as well. In October her grandson Prince Christian Victor of Schleswig-Holstein died of fever while serving in South Africa, and his sister Marie Louise's unhappy marriage was annulled. Christmas 1900 was saddened by the death of Queen Victoria's devoted friend and lady-in-waiting, Jane Churchill. On 17 January 1901 the queen suffered a mild stroke, and the family were summoned to her bedside at Osborne. Five days later she died, thus ending a reign of sixty-three years, her last audible word being 'Bertie'.

With her passing, Emperor Francis Joseph was unquestionably the senior crowned head of Europe. He had reigned over his empire for fifty-two years, and despite internal dissension and a series of military defeats, he had acquired experience and prestige which could not be matched by any of his fellow-monarchs. The other two doomed empires, Germany and Russia, were presided over respectively by an unstable megalomaniac (Emperor William II) and a kind-hearted yet unhappily indecisive family man (Tsar Nicholas II). King Leopold II of the Belgians, King George I of Greece and his father King Christian IX of Denmark had each worn their crowns for over thirty-five years, but though their monarchies were stable enough neither Belgium nor Denmark could be regarded as major continental powers, while the kingdom of Greece was hardly a model of stability.

Though King Edward VII was aged fifty-nine and in indifferent health when he ascended the British throne, he soon established a reputation which fulfilled the promise he had shown as prince of Wales. His political knowledge of the European courts and their leading personalities, plus his tactful manner, belied the image created by his censorious critics of an ageing card-sharper with scant respect for the commandment relating to adultery.

In 1901 there was no close relationship between the most important Protestant and the greatest Catholic court in Europe. Such tenuous political sympathies that had existed died with Crown Prince Rudolf. The judgment of one recent biographer that Francis Joseph had never liked Albert Edward as prince of Wales and cared for him even less as king is somewhat extreme.[2] What can be said with certainty was that both men, despite a mere eleven years' difference in age, were too dissimilar in outlook and personality to be close friends. The seventy-year-old emperor, with his courteous old-fashioned manner, lack of interest in dazzling uniforms, who slept in a tiny room furnished only with an iron bedstead and washstand, found the younger man's pleasure-loving existence and ready acceptance of rich, amusing Jews and Americans as companions, hard to comprehend. Moreover, his relationship with Rudolf was an ever-present reminder of the bitter events of 1889. But emperor and king respected each other warmly and genuinely wished to trust each other in the interests of European peace and stability.

When Britain's stock had fallen throughout Europe during the Boer war which had overshadowed Queen Victoria's last fifteen months, Francis Joseph had been almost alone in Austria – if not on the continent – in expressing sympathy for the British point of view. At a court ball, he had declared in the presence of foreign diplomats, that with regard to the war he was completely English. King Edward felt himself ever in the emperor's debt as a result.

As a prelude to closer Anglo-Austrian relations, Edward VII paid his first (and in fact his only) visit to Vienna as king in 1903. It was indeed the first appearance of an English king in Austria since Richard I had been careless enough to be captured and interned at Durrenstein on his return from Jerusalem in 1192.

Leaving Marienbad for the capital on 31 August, the king lost no time in giving proof of his tact and imagination. At a banquet at the Hofburg on his first evening, he delighted his astonished host by announcing his appointment as field-marshal of the British army. The gift in itself was not surprising, for the emperor was already an honorary Colonel of the 1st King's Dragoon Guards of ten years' standing. What was startling was the way in which it was conferred. According to custom, such appointments concerning foreign rulers were notified to those rulers' capitals and cleared with military authorities at home well in advance. King Edward cared little for such tedious niceties, and with his knowledge of human nature he believed that such a gift would be far more effective if bestowed unexpectedly. He was correct, for the emperor was thrilled. He could talk of little else for the rest of the evening. One of his priorities early next morning was to send personal telegrams of greeting to all fellow field-marshals in the British army list. The emperor's personal staff had rarely seen their master unbend so much. To them, the king of England had achieved the impossible.

To the prince of Wales, later King George V, King Edward wrote (5 September):

> Nothing could have gone off better than my visit to Vienna. The Emperor was as usual kindness itself – and I had an excellent reception from the people generally – who are not demonstrative but wonderfully orderly – No troops in the streets – as they are all at the manoeuvres . . . I went out shooting with the Emperor on Wednesday, . . . and killed a very fine stag with very wide horns. . .[3]

But private conversations between monarchs soon revealed the limits of the king's miraculous powers. He had two matters to raise with the emperor.

The first was a purely personal family subject, the plight of the former crown princess of Austria-Hungary. Since Rudolf's death, Stephanie had been treated as a virtual outcast by her father, who was hated throughout Europe not only for his infamous treatment of his family but also on account of atrocities in the Congo carried out in his name. When she made a second, happier marriage in 1900 to the Hungarian aristocrat Prince Elmer Lonyay, King Leopold declared it to be incompatible with his dignity and promptly cut her out of his will. Francis Joseph had never liked his daughter-in-law, though it was inconceivable to imagine him stooping to such spiteful depths as the notoriously miserly king of the Belgians. Could His Imperial Majesty, King Edward asked, perhaps write to King Leopold or make some gesture to intervene on Princess Lonyay's behalf? Although nothing seems to have resulted, it was a kind move well in keeping with the king's character.

The other subject of discussion which King Edward raised was the sultan of Turkey's ill-treatment of his Christian subjects in Macedonia, and general instability in the Ottoman empire. He wished for some pressure to be applied to the sultan, and was impatient at the great powers' apparent disinterest. Before leaving Vienna he also mentioned it to Count Goluchowski, urging on him a determined yet peaceful attitude towards Turkey in the Balkans. To the minister, he commented that Anglo-Austrian policy was virtually identical, as he saw it – namely to preserve the status quo in the Near East as long as possible, and thus avoid a war which would have incalculable consequences for Europe. As long as

Austria did nothing provocative in the Balkans, she could count on England's support.

After establishing this measure of close personal contact which had been quite unknown in Queen Victoria's reign, King Edward was determined to make it last. One way in which he felt this was best done was to consult the emperor on relatively uncontroversial topics which were of close interest to him. Early in 1904 he asked the military attache at the British embassy in Vienna to enquire from the emperor his views about arming cavalry with lances. He made it clear that he wanted the emperor's private opinion, as opposed to what leading military circles in Vienna were thinking.

Francis Joseph was flattered that King Edward should ask his views in this way, and replied warmly with a very long letter setting out the pros and cons of equipping cavalry with lances and the possible implications on modern warfare. The way was thus paved for the regular interchange of ideas on similar matters.

Both sovereigns arranged for their heirs to visit each others' courts. During the spring of 1904, the prince and princess of Wales were entertained at the Hofburg. Their reception at the Vienna railway station, on 18 April, was 'most alarming', according to Princess May. Waiting to greet them were not only the emperor himself, but several archdukes, members of the British embassy, and a guard of honour. Their arrival at the Hofburg was 'another ordeal', for all the Austrian archdukes stood at the head of the staircases. The prince and princess had to say a word to each, but the latter found it 'all delightful tho' tiring, everyone so kind and the Emperor charming'. They were allotted the use of twelve apartments, and dined with the Austrian suite attached to them and their own household, finding the emperor's timetable of dining at five and retiring to bed at eight not quite their style.

During their four days in Vienna they were treated to the usual round of balls, supper-parties and opera house visits. One of the princess's ladies-in-waiting, Lady Mary Lygon, found the archduchesses very stiff, 'so everyone raved over the ease and charm of the Princess's manners.'[4] They attended a large luncheon party at Schönbrunn, where she carefully examined every room of the palace, and drove around the grounds with the emperor in a *pirutchade*, a small carriage about two hundred years old. She made the most of her visit, sightseeing in Vienna, which as she observed ruefully made a strange contrast with the one highlight of her husband's activities, a capercaillie shoot in the country.

On a subsequent visit to Paris, she enthused over art treasures and historical buildings as she had in Vienna:

> With all my love of history you can imagine what a pleasure all this has been to me, alas for my poor George all these things are a sealed

book, such a pity & so deplorable in his position! & he misses so much that is interesting in one's life.[5]

Prince George's comment on their Viennese sojourn was typically terse: 'Everybody most kind and nice but my goodness this Court is stiff and they are frightened of the Emperor'.[6]

The Austrian heir was likewise paying periodic visits to Britain. Archduke Francis Ferdinand's appearance at the diamond jubilee of Queen Victoria had been followed by another, representing the emperor, at her funeral in 1901. He also attended King Edward's coronation in August 1902, and the monarch duly appointed him a Knight Companion of the Garter.

These exchanges were formal in the extreme, and there seems to have been little if any close personal contact between king and archduke. The former probably assumed that, all things being equal, he would soon see the day when he would congratulate Emperor Francis Ferdinand on his accession, and under normal circumstances he would doubtless have tried to cultivate some form of acquaintance with the future emperor.

But one complication stood in the way. Francis Ferdinand had had the temerity to fall in love with a lady-in-waiting at the Austrian court, Countess Sophie Chotek. Although she came from a respected imperial family (her father, as ambassador to Brussels, had been largely responsible for negotiating the ill-starred marriage between Rudolf and Stephanie), her rank was insufficient for that of a future empress of Austria-Hungary. In spite of wrath and indignation from all sides, the archduke tenaciously refused to give her up. At length he was permitted to marry her morganatically, on condition that he renounced all royal and imperial rights for her and for their issue. Sophie was created princess of Hohenberg on their wedding in June 1900, but otherwise the stiff Habsburg protocol saw to it that she was treated with every humiliation possible at court, being denied all rights due to an archduchess.

To her credit Sophie conducted herself with dignity and patience. This, and Francis Ferdinand's obvious devotion to her and their three children, won respect from all but the most heartless. The legend that Emperor Francis Joseph despised them and never forgave his nephew for besmirching the Habsburg dynasty with a morganatic marriage is one that has persisted to this day. In private he showed them every kindness possible, but in public he could never unbend; a countess could not be accorded the same precedence or privileges as an archduchess. It was a problem which perplexed every European monarch in turn, though in England, according to Henry Wickham

Steed,* it was considered only natural that Sophie should be recognised as empress on her husband's accession.

After his appointment as field-marshal, the emperor conferred the rank of Austro-Hungarian field-marshal on King Edward VII, and sent Archduke Frederick to England to take him his new uniform. Nonetheless Francis Joseph stubbornly declined all invitations to come to London. Because of the unwritten rules of royal etiquette, this prevented the king from making a second visit to Vienna.

As a result, a system of informal meetings developed between the sovereigns that summer at the spas of Marienbad and Bad Ischl. King Edward now had such a reputation for mixing politics with pleasure that it was widely believed he was trying to draw the emperor away from his traditional alliance with Germany. Out of this arose Germany's view that the king was mainly responsible for the outbreak of war in 1914 on account of his attempts to encircle imperial Germany with hostile alliances.

King Edward had first been to Marienbad as prince of Wales in 1897. Under his patronage it soon became a bustling royal resort, and he made a practice of staying at the Hotel Weimar under the incognito of duke of Lancaster. The assumption of such titles owed more to a royal sense of whimsical humour than any genuine desire to conceal identity, for the name 'duke of Lancaster' did no more to convince hotel staff or locals than the appellation 'countess of Balmoral' had for his late mother on her European travels.

Marienbad attracted not only royalty but also eminent politicians and others from public life. How convincing the 'cure' was for its patrons is open to doubt. The king's equerry, Sir Frederick Ponsonby, remarked that he had never seen so many fat people anywhere else.

The first of these meetings took place in August 1904. The king, attired in his Austrian field-marshal's uniform, waited on the station platform with a small suite to greet the emperor on his arrival. After embracing warmly, both sovereigns drove to their respective quarters through triumphal arches festooned with Habsburg double-headed eagles and British lions and unicorns. The city fathers had spared neither effort nor expense in decorating the town and hotel apartments for their distinguished guests. Unaware of the emperor's spartan habits and his military field bed at Schönbrunn, they had purchased a magnificent bed of English brass for him to sleep in.

However, King Edward's dignified informality seemed to have a good effect on the emperor at dinner that night at the Hotel Weimar. He had arranged every detail of the menu himself, including grouse sent from Scotland where the shooting season had just begun. There

* *The Times* correspondent in Vienna, 1902–13.

were no long tedious speeches, just short unrehearsed toasts between king and emperor. As with the visit to Vienna in 1903, Francis Joseph's entourage noticed that their master seemed to unbend perceptibly in the king's presence, appearing much more relaxed than he did at home.

The meeting was of no great historical importance, though courtiers and journalists tried to assume it was at the time. Rumours that Edward took the opportunity to try and start weaning Austria away from her alliance with Germany, by persuading the emperor to settle Balkan affairs in Europe's favour while Russia was distracted by her war with Japan at the time, were unfounded. But in the same way that the king had helped to create a favourable political atmosphere by his very successful visit to France earlier in his reign, a France which had not quite forgiven or forgotten Britain's responsibility for the Boer war, he was laying foundations for what might well be harmonious relations between London and Vienna.

Austrian reaction to the conclusion of the Entente Cordiale between Britain and France in April 1904, like that throughout most of Europe, was generally favourable. The *Neue Frei Presse* of Vienna commented that no unease need be felt over its signing. Although Germany might be expected to complain that her colonial ambitions would be thus curbed, a signal service to the cause of world peace had been rendered. The Russo-Japanese war would be contained and threat of conflict between the ever-mutually suspicious Britain and Russia (officially recognised as a French ally since the end of the nineteenth century) would be substantially reduced. In short, the paper commended King Edward's 'far-seeing wisdom' and acknowledged his efforts in bringing the Entente Cordiale into being. The king's peaceful intentions were thus recognised by Austria; only in the German empire was he suspected of encirclement.

The contrast between the courts at Windsor and Vienna was always apparent. By the Edwardian era, a vast gulf between the two was evident. Recalling her visit to Austria of 1904 some forty years later, Queen Mary remarked in private conversation that the collapse of the imperial systems in Austria and Russia had come as no surprise to her, since she could never understand how such an inflexible and hierarchical order, so totally detached from the people of those countries, could possibly survive in a free and modern world.[7]

Members of the suite which accompanied King Edward to Marienbad were likewise both amused and perplexed at what they termed the 'compartmentalisation' of Austrian court life. The informality of Edwardian society had its limits, but beside the regimented Habsburg etiquette it must have appeared positively slapdash. At Marienbad, they were privileged to watch no less than nineteen separate groups, in strict sequence of protocol, line up to present their respects to the sovereign. First came the aristocracy, in order themselves according to lineage, followed by army officers, municipal authorities, and other groups, war veterans and the fire brigades bringing up the rear. The English could not help but feel that a society which existed on such rigid lines would be rent asunder at the merest sign of change from the outside world. England's court had moved with the times, to the dismay of a few old-fashioned critics who still yearned for the dignified austerity of Queen Victoria's day, and looked askance on the free-and-easy regime of her eldest son. That of Austria still appeared frozen in time.

In August 1905 the rendezvous took place at Bad Ischl, the emperor's summer residence in the mountains surrounded by game forests. It was on this occasion that the king was supposed to have furthered his attempts to entice Austria away from her German sympathies. According to Margutti, King Edward offered

> compensation in a form that was certainly very enticing. Its very attractiveness made it incumbent on the old Emperor to proceed with the greatest caution and reserve, and thus his conversation with the King during this long drive – a conversation full of pitfalls – became nothing less than an ordeal.[8]

Margutti was not present on this carriage drive from Ischl to Halstatt, and nowhere does he specify or even hint what the 'enticing compensation' may have been. All he adds is that his master returned quite broken and worn out, and at dinner that night seemed on the verge of collapse.

A rather different and probably more reliable view of the afternoon's proceedings came from King Edward himself, who wrote to Sir Ernest Cassel (17 August) that he and the emperor 'had some very interesting conversations. Would to God that some other sovereigns were as sensible as he is!'[9]

August 1907 was the month of what was recognised at the time as an Anglo-Austrian summit meeting. In July, King Edward set the wheels in motion. He announced to Count Albert von Mensdorff,* Austrian ambassador at London since 1904, that if the emperor was agreeable he would like to bring Charles Hardinge of the foreign office, and the new Austrian minister of the exterior, Baron Alois Aehrenthal, ought to be there as well; sovereigns and statesmen could therefore meet.

The plan was approved in Vienna, and the king had a lengthy conversation with Mensdorff as to the subjects for discussion. Among

---

* Son of Count Alexander von Mensdorff.

them was the ever-pressing problem of Macedonia. King Edward and his ministers firmly believed that Turkish ill-treatment of the Christians must be forcibly stopped if racial and religious violence was to cease – otherwise it could threaten peace in the Balkans, and perhaps erupt into European war. Austria, on the other hand, appeared to favour a policy of *laissez-faire*. As the Habsburg monarchy shared a southern frontier with the Balkans, Austria-Hungary would have to contend with any instability and possible collapse of the Ottoman empire.

The Habsburg family and imperial ministers gathered each July and August at the Kaiservilla, a sprawling yellow-washed house at Bad Ischl, given to the emperor as a wedding present. It was here that the king and Hardinge arrived on 15 August, after a relatively satisfactory meeting with the German emperor at Kronberg.

The greeting given these august visitors was in stark contrast to that experienced by King Edward and Hardinge at Cassel the previous day, a martial parade of 50,000 soldiers lining the streets. At Ischl, the carriage containing king and emperor was welcomed by crowds of men from the voluntary fire services, workers from the salt mines, and two hundred girls dressed in traditional peasant *dirndl* who pelted the vehicle with small bouquets of alpine flowers. Also lining the streets, in a less official capacity, were hordes of school children, and English and American holidaymakers. The only concession to formality was represented by twelve gendarmes giving a salute. King Edward's delight at this village carnival-like atmosphere, which his German nephew would have probably regarded as being beneath his dignity, can easily be imagined.

The carriage stopped at the Hotel Elizabeth, where the king was presented with a bouquet by the small daughter of the hotel proprietor, Herr Seeauer. He was so impressed by this that he swung the child in his arms and kissed her on both cheeks.

At lunch Aehrenthal and Hardinge renewed their acquaintance (each had previously met at St Petersburg while serving as ambassadors for their respective countries) while emperor and king went on a carriage drive on their own afterwards. This was done on the emperor's suggestion, and hardly bore out Margutti's assertion that he was by now dreading Edward's one-man conspiracy to entice him away from the German alliance. When they returned, the emperor had a private conversation with Hardinge, while the king and Aehrenthal had a similar meeting.

In the evening, a performance of a Strauss operetta was staged in the king's honour. After supper both monarchs went for a carriage drive around the town, bathed in moonlight and lit by the glow of thousands of lamps, torches and three hundred mountain fires specially lit on the peaks above.

The fine weather lasted just long enough. King Edward left for Marienbad the following morning, having embraced the emperor warmly, on a railway station drenched with rain.

This relaxed setting had made for an extremely harmonious series of meetings. It was announced at the time that 'complete accord' had been reached by both powers with regard to their policy towards Macedonia and the Balkans, on reforms to be launched in the province and on measures to be introduced to fight terrorism and persecution. Though it was by no means a permanent arrangement and no treaties or agreements had been signed, the air had been cleared between Britain and Austria. In recognition of his part in the proceedings, on the morning of his departure from Ischl it was announced that the king had bestowed on Aehrenthal the Grand Cross of the Royal Victorian Order. Mensdorff noted approvingly in his diary that he was very happy at how splendidly everything had gone: 'May the good Lord help things further along so that A(ehrenthal) loses his distrust of England and that they get used to him at the F.O.'[10]

Above all, there was no distrust in Germany of English motives as might have been expected. After King Edward's very successful visits to Kronberg, relations between England and Germany were good for once, and Aehrenthal had told Hardinge how he and Austria rejoiced in this development. German diplomats meanwhile quoted the king as saying that any weakening of the age-old Austro-German alliance would be a great misfortune. Suddenly relations between the main European powers, normally so highly charged with mutual distrust, appeared uncannily if not deceptively peaceful.

Hardinge reported to Sir Edward Grey, foreign secretary, that there appeared to be a degree of tension behind the laughing and joking between King Edward and Emperor William. However, the king's relations with Emperor Francis Joseph appeared to him to be 'of the most friendly and intimate character. They seemed to delight in each other's company and were practically inseparable. . .'[11]

By 1908, Anglo-German relations had deteriorated again as a result of Germany's rapid shipbuilding programme. The next meeting at Bad Ischl therefore took place against a rather strained atmosphere, complicated by evident mutual suspicion between Grey and Aehrenthal. (As Mensdorff had commented ruefully after discussing the expedition with King Edward in April, there was no doubt that 'our Aehrenthal rubs people up the wrong way'[12]).

The king expressed a wish to Vienna to make the occasion as festive as possible, as it coincided with the emperor's diamond jubilee year. The latter suggested that proceedings should take place at Vienna, with a state banquet at Schönbrunn. When Mensdorff put this to the king, he turned the idea down, for political and personal reasons. He recognised that Emperor William would be suspicious at a second visit by his rival to Vienna as sovereign, when Emperor Francis Joseph had not been to London and appeared unlikely to at his venerable age; and, as King Edward always went to Marienbad in August, Ischl, being on the way, was more convenient and certainly more comfortable.

Emperor William's suspicions had indeed been aroused in no uncertain manner. He had therefore been quick to take advantage of diamond jubilee year. In May 1908, he led a deputation of all princes from the federation (except for the grand duke of Hesse, who declined to participate) to Schönbrunn. Together they presented Germany's congratulations to Emperor Francis Joseph on his anniversary, and William's speech, it was said, was 'a declaration of allegiance almost unprecedented in its sincerity and eloquence'.[13]

In his biography of the Austrian emperor, Redlich commented more fully on 'this wholly unique and by no means merely formal homage' devised by Emperor William:

> In it Francis Joseph saw a supreme form of recognition of the German-Austrian Alliance as the golden bridge between past and future for the empires it bound together. He knew a moment of grateful respite from the anxious thought of the dangers threatening his realm from within and without.[14]

Anxious thoughts there doubtless were in London on this occasion.

Small wonder, therefore, that August 1908 saw no repetition of the previous summer's success. The king's train drew up at Ischl station in pouring rain to a platform lined by soldiers in uniform. Perhaps Francis Joseph felt that the informality of last time had been mocked in Berlin, and that his diamond jubilee required something rather more solemn. Many other people had tried to get on the platform to welcome His Majesty on his arrival at 9.45 a.m. Early that morning, the stationmaster noticed that an unprecedented number of tickets had been sold for trains due to leave Ischl between ten and eleven that morning. As a precaution, all normal passenger services were immediately suspended and the station cleared by police soon after nine o'clock.

However, political conversations held after lunch seemed more promising. Aehrenthal, it was considered, appeared more amenable and understanding over the Macedonian question. The situation had been transformed by a revolt in July 1908 of the 'young Turks' against the sultan's oppressive rule, and there was a distinct possibility of reforms in the sultan's Balkan domains being settled by new and more liberal measures enforced by the Turks themselves.

Once again, while ministers and diplomats were engrossed in their own discussions, the emperor suggested a carriage ride to the king.

They had been talking about automobiles (among more pressing subjects), then a new form of transport to which King Edward was no stranger. He noticed a few, belonging to distinguished visitors, driving around the village. This was evidently the moment, he felt. for his host to try one out for the first time. After much persuasion. Francis Jossph was prevailed upon to ride in a Züst, a German–Belgian car belonging to his son-in-law Prince Leopold of Bavaria. King Edward eagerly asked the emperor to climb aboard the vehicle first. 'No, no, you go ahead,' the elder man allegedly insisted, 'you know more about it.' Although it was mid-August and the weather had suddenly cleared up, he was provided with a blanket in case it should be too chilly for him. His daughter Gisela offered him cotton wool for his ears to drown the engine's roar, as she and Leopold climbed aboard to sit behind the two sovereigns. The drive to Weissenbach lasted eighty minutes, and at one point they attained the magnificent speed of 20 m.p.h.

Legend would have one believe that King Edward took this opportunity to discuss his main objective with the emperor – namely, to ask him to try and bring some pressure to bear on the German emperor to curb his shipbuilding programme. This is very unlikely. The king would hardly have raised such a contentious subject on what was intended to be a pleasure trip – though such a term is perhaps inappropriate in view of the seventy-seven year-old emperor's feeling of nervousness at experiencing the dubious excitement of motoring for the very first time. Moreover, even if he was not making full use of his borrowed cotton wool, they were not alone, being accompanied by Prince and Princess Leopold and the chauffeur. King Edward was the last person on earth to broach such a confidential matter in front of others.

However, King Edward did raise the matter that day, probably after they returned from the drive. All that is known for certain is that he received a polite but unequivocal refusal to his request for Austrian pressure on Berlin. It is said that the emperor excused himself from any such obligation with the words, 'After all, I am a German prince,' but the fact that the main authority for this statement was the emperor's valet, who allegedly heard it from a ghillie on a deer stalking expedition at Ischl, makes it improbable. His Imperial Majesty was too sensible a monarch to mention such matters to a servant.

But he had perfectly sound reasons for declining to approach Emperor William to this effect. The Austro-German alliance had been the main pillar of Francis Joseph's foreign policy for thirty years, and he would not do anything to threaten this. Moreover, the unwritten code of imperial conduct would have forbidden him to interfere by questioning a brother sovereign on his defence policy and armed forces. Though King Edward recognised this, he must have hoped for some vague ministerial intercession by Viennese statesmen on their Berlin counterparts, something which Francis Joseph would not promise as he could not guarantee to deliver.

There were technical reasons besides. The emperor knew much less than the king about naval affairs, and was totally uninterested, leaving them entirely to Archduke Francis Ferdinand. Even the king's knowledge was limited, in spite of his enthusiasm for a strong English fleet. It is unlikely that he knew, during the very same week, that the first Austro-Hungarian navy air pilots were receiving their initial training in England.

There are surviving accounts of how the monarchs' closest confidantes tackled this issue with each other. Hardinge later wrote that he had pointed out to Aehrenthal that Austria, as Germany's ally, could make a significant contribution to European peace by acting as a brake on any ambitious naval policy the government in Berlin intended to pursue. Aehrenthal admitted to him that the second Reich's attitude threatened to precipitate a very critical Anglo-German situation which it was in the interests of other nations to avoid. As a friend, he wished to tell Hardinge in confidence that he had received indications of a mood in Germany which was strongly opposed to the national naval programme. This, and the pressing financial problems of the government, were both growing at a pace which might make it necessary for German ministers to curtail their naval expansion accordingly.

The Austrian view of events was recorded by Mensdorff, who wrote in rather more blunt terms. English approaches to achieve some understanding with Germany over her naval programme, he maintained, were rejected with regret. He echoed Hardinge's comments that Aehrenthal had mentioned how the pace of German naval armaments could not be increased because of the cost in terms of finance and public opinion. Nonetheless, Austria was a loyal ally of Germany and intended to remain so. There could be no question of her taking any part in Anglo-German arguments over their fleet.

Most importantly, Mensdorff noted that Aehrenthal had spoken firmly in this vein to Hardinge and the king, and 'met with understanding'. This makes nonsense of assertions that King Edward attempted to destroy the Austro-German alliance, and left in a bad temper after failing to do so. While this Ischl meeting could not be regarded as an unqualified success from the English point of view, both parties left on amicable terms, having agreed to differ, and respect each others' views. The king departed for Marienbad after a very cordial farewell from Francis Joseph. Hardinge and Mensdorff each gave their verdicts that the meetings had been 'entirely satisfactory.'

From Marienbad, King Edward wrote to Sir Ernest Cassel, one of the few friends on whose discretion he relied implicitly. He mentioned that Sir Charles Hardinge had discussed the naval question at Kronberg with Emperor William, who 'did not see his way to diminish his shipbuilding programme', a source of English regret as it left them with no alternative but to pursue their own naval expansion. As for the Austrian visit and his exchanges with Emperor Francis Joseph, he only mentioned that the latter was 'much interested as well as agitated' over news from the Balkans, and that he greatly enjoyed his first ride in a motor car, 'and will I hope in the future not object to that mode of locomotion'.[15]

The king was apparently not at all discouraged over his lack of success at this stage. Neither he nor the foreign office intended to leave things as they stood. There was a tacit agreement between them to try and gently reduce Austria's supposed subservience to Germany, not merely for selfish British motives, but more generally as a step towards preserving peace throughout Europe. According to Crozier, French ambassador at Vienna, despite the cordiality of personal relations between king and emperor, their meeting produced no political results – yet:

> The Emperor of Austria did not feel able to intervene with his ally on the delicate question of [naval] armaments. . .King Edward is said to have aimed at achieving at least a modification in the political line of the Monarchy. . .He will certainly try again. . .[16]

'The old Emperor is the dearest and most courteous old gentleman that lives,' Hardinge glowingly informed Knollys, the king's equerry.

On 15 August 1908, two days after the king had arrived at Marienbad, came an indication that they had spoken a little too optimistically. Wickham Steed, who was adept at knowing what was about to happen on the European political scene, had some remarkable news for His Majesty. Austria was on the point, he told King Edward, of preparing to annex the provinces of Bosnia and Herzegovina.

The king did not believe him. Such a move, he said, would throw the whole of Europe into alarm. Moreover the Austrian emperor had given him no hint that anything of the sort might happen. Steed was adamant, citing as his source an unnamed senior Austrian official who had approached him on behalf of the imperial cabinet to find out English reaction to the plan. But the king would still have none of it, insisting that 'surely the Emperor would have said something to me'.

The king had every right to be astonished by his fellow-monarch's silence on the subject. One can only suppose that the autocrat of the 1850s had become such a model of constitutional monarchy by 1908 that control of events had been well and truly taken out of his grasp. The other possibility is that he felt the matter to be none of King

Edward's business, though how aware he was of the annexation proposals must be left to speculation. All that is known for certain is that it was a mere three days after Steed's warning – on the emperor's seventy-eighth birthday, 18 August 1908 – that the joint council of Austrian and Hungarian ministers in Vienna took the decision to annex the provinces.

The timing gave some credence to the impression that it was intended as a diamond jubilee birthday present for the emperor, but that was certainly not the only reason. During his long and hardly glorious reign, the Austrian nation had suffered a severe loss of prestige in her expulsion from Italy in the south, and her removal from the German confederation in the north. Only in the south-east could she still dare risk any form of territorial expansion, at the expense of the ailing Turkish empire. She also wished to absorb the two states in order to prevent them from being acquired in a similar manner by her unpredictable rival and neighbour Serbia.

Not until 29 September did Francis Joseph write personally to the other European monarchs and heads of state, notifying them of this decision:

> I am anxious to warn you personally of an important decision which I shall soon see myself obliged to take and which you will judge – I am sure – in the spirit of close and traditional friendship which binds us together.
>
> It concerns a problem to which the solution cannot be deferred without danger for the peaceful development of events close to the frontiers of my Empire.
>
> The fate of Bosnia and Herzegovina had been entrusted in 1878 on the initiative of the British delegates, to Austria-Hungary with the objective of establishing there "a stable and strong admin- istration". These provinces have since attained, thanks to the assiduous care of my government, a high degree of material and intellectual culture; they therefore aspire legitimately to the benefits of an autonomous and constitutional regime that my Government does not believe it can refuse any longer in the light of unforeseen events which have come to pass in Turkey.
>
> Now, it does not appear possible to proceed to the concession of a constitution for Bosnia and Herzegovina before having established in a definitive manner the political situation of these provinces.
>
> These are not therefore considerations of political expediency, but pressing requirements of the situation which will oblige me to proceed with the annexation of Bosnia and Herzegovina.
>
> I must be careful to add that the decision which I shall see myself obliged to take will not alter at all the conservative

political direction of the politics of Austria-Hungary and that my government will also observe in future the principles of disinterest which it has established many a time.

It is with these ideas in mind that I have authorised my government to renounce at the moment of the annexation of Bosnia and Herzegovina, to the exercise of military and administrative rights that the treaty of Berlin has conferred on us in the Sandjak of Novibazar. The immediate recall of my troops which at present maintain a garrison will emphasise this renunciation.[17]

King Edward was horrified. Such a move threatened the peace of Europe, as Austria had traditionally been relied on since the congress of Berlin to help maintain some form of stability in the troubled Balkans. Not only this, but the emperor had said nothing to him, and thought it inconceivable that he could have entertained him at Ischl without giving any hint that such policy was under consideration.

To add insult to injury, the king did not receive his copy of the letter until it was delivered to him by Mensdorff at Balmoral on the afternoon of 5 October. The ambassador had been instructed to keep it until that date. The Austro-Hungarian ambassador in Paris had received similar orders not to present his copy of the letter to the president of the French republic until the same time, but ignored his orders and handed it over two days earlier.

On that same day, 3 October, Mensdorff saw Hardinge at the foreign office and handed him a private letter from Aehrenthal, announcing the Austrian government's intention to proclaim the annexation very shortly. Mensdorff added that he was the bearer of a private letter from Emperor Francis Joseph to King Edward VII, making a formal announcement of the news. Hardinge immediately telegraphed to the king to warn him beforehand.

When Mensdorff reached Balmoral with the famous letter, he found the atmosphere distinctly chilly. Already aware of its contents, the king received him coldly and scanned it as a formality. He felt it a gross breach of confidence, and discourtesy on the emperor's part, for such a private letter to be conveyed through an ambassador. Mensdorff was dismissed with a few curt words.

Lord Redesdale, who was then staying at Balmoral, later commented in his memoirs that nobody present could forget how terribly upset the king was – 'never did I see him so moved'.

He regarded the emperor's silence on the matter at Ischl as almost tantamount to a breach of faith. Had Austria, he wondered, consulted Turkey, who had nominally owned the provinces? What would Russia, who had more than a passing interest in the Balkans, make of it? Why had Aehrenthal deliberately lied to Goschen, British ambassador in Berlin, by assuring him that same week that there were no proposals to annex them?

The following week, Goschen called upon Aehrenthal and taxed him formally with lying. The Austrian minister attempted to deny it, but Goschen was not fooled. Before leaving Vienna for Berlin, they attended a dinner given by the emperor in honour of King George of Greece. Aehrenthal complained indignantly to Goschen of hostility in the British press over the annexation, saying that England was thus incurring 'a very heavy responsibility'. Goschen defended himself on behalf of his country by stating that responsibility lay with Austria, who had annexed Bosnia and Herzegovina in defiance of the treaty of Berlin. Aehrenthal's reaction was to denounce angrily British conduct during the Boer war, but Goschen won the argument by pointing out that the war in South Africa had nothing to do with the matter. Moreover, Britain had not violated an international treaty. 'That is the truth; but you, my dear Minister, do not love the truth.'[18]

Tactfully, but with a heavy heart, King Edward wrote to the emperor (10 October):

> I have just received the letter in which you have warned me of the important decision that you have taken to proceed with the annexation of Bosnia and Herzegovina, and I must thank you for having thought to acquaint me with your views in a manner so befitting to our friendship.
>
> However I cannot help conveying to you my deepest regrets at seeing such a decision being taken, above all at a time when developments in Bulgaria have already compromised the situation in the Balkan states.*
>
> Nor will I conceal from you how much I adhere to the sacred principles enshrined in the Protocol of 17 January 1871 according to which the treaty of Berlin cannot be modified without the consent of the Contracting Powers, and above all, in this actual case, of Turkey, which is the most interested Power.
>
> I learn with pleasure that your decision taken in the circumstances will not alter at all the conservative orientation of the politics of Austria-Hungary. . .[19]

King Edward felt so bitterly about the affair that, early in 1909, he wished to express his disapproval by refusing to invite Mensdorff to Windsor again. It took all Hardinge's powers of persuasion to prevent his master from taking such drastic action. If Mensdorff was to be the only European ambassador not invited to the castle, there would be indignant attacks on His Majesty in the Austrian press.

---

* Two days before Austria's formal announcement of the annexation, Prince Ferdinand of Bulgaria had startled Europe by proclaiming Bulgarian independence from Turkish sovereignty, and assuming the title of tsar.

Nonetheless there was criticism of England's diplomatic support for Serbia, who felt herself threatened by the annexation. The official opinion, in Austrian newspapers at least, was that King Edward was personally supporting the cause of Serbia out of spite, after failing to separate Austria from her time-honoured alliance with Germany. Mensdorff, known cynically in Vienna as 'Royal Albert', was considered by Aehrenthal to be so pro-British that he was incapable of safeguarding Austria's interests.

On 2 December 1908, Emperor Francis Joseph celebrated the completion of his sixtieth year on the throne.

To many people, not least himself, those six eventful decades must have seemed an eternity. He had been appointed, rather than succeeded, to the throne at a time of acute continental crisis. Wars had been fought and lost, the German confederation had become but a distant memory, his closest relations had been taken from him more often than not in circumstances of cruel tragedy, and once again an European crisis was threatening.

In London the anniversary was commemorated by the Austro-Hungarian colony with a high-mass thanksgiving celebrated at the Church of the Immaculate Conception, Farm Street, in Berkeley Square. The king and the prince of Wales, it was reported, 'were represented', and in the evening a banquet for three hundred guests was given under the presidency of the Austro-Hungarian ambassador. One would imagine that King Edward and his heir might have attended in person had the diamond jubilee fallen a year or even months earlier, but the sovereign was still reeling from his former friend's behaviour. In his blackest moods, he feared that Francis Joseph was becoming just as aggressive as the German emperor, or at least losing control of his ministers and their foreign policy. Such a move as the annexation was the kind of action that William II, whose impulsive behaviour had already provoked one or two crises that had alarmed Europe, might be expected to take. But surely not the courteous, dignified, more experienced monarch from Vienna? Even William had been offended at not being taken into his ally's confidence, though not enough to feel that ties binding their empires had been weakened at all.

According to Joseph Redlich, parliamentarian and the most reliable of Francis Joseph's biographers, British hostility towards Austria distressed the emperor acutely, as he had always attached great importance to good relations with the British government. Evidently some of Rudolf's admiration of parliamentary democracy after the Westminster fashion had rubbed off on him, as he remarked to Redlich in the course of conversation that the English were the most intelligent and efficient politicians, for they always managed to achieve a good compromise between parties. 'How different from us in Austria!'[20]

The aftermath of the annexation crisis lasted until spring 1909. In April, Turkey was paid a heavy sum in compensation for losing on paper the provinces she had not possessed since the treaty of Berlin. Serbia had imagined herself absorbing Bosnia and Herzegovina into a new Southern Slav bloc under her control, and demanded compensation as well. There were fears that Russia would support her, and even the possibility that Austrian troops might march on Belgrade and annex the Serbian capital. Only after Germany had dissuaded Russia from open support for Serbia, and after Sir Edward Grey had assisted in making the settlement, did Serbia accept the situation.

But armed conflict had become a chillingly close prospect. Aehrenthal, King Edward declared, was 'the devil incarnate'. In May the king asked his prime minister Asquith whether the cabinet had taken into consideration 'the possible (but the King hopes improbable) event of a European war'[21] when preparing the budget.

Presumably as a gesture to show he bore no lasting ill-will towards Austria, he still took his annual cure at Marienbad in August 1909. Not to do so would have caused adverse comment and engendered deep suspicion on the continent.

On 11 August he arrived at the Weimar hotel, and was immediately handed a telegram of welcome from the emperor. Though he did his best to avoid any political contacts, he entertained Clemenceau, former prime minister of France, and Crozier to luncheon after divine service on Sunday, 15 August. Three days later, on the emperor's seventy-ninth birthday, he sent a bust of himself and a letter of congratulation to Francis Joseph. In the morning he attended a *Te Deum* in the Roman Catholic church, received a company of Austrian officers who were also taking the waters at Marienbad, and in the evening he gave a banquet in the emperor's honour.

King Edward returned to London in the first week of September. Though his sojourn at Marienbad had passed off satisfactorily enough, the previous year's events had made it far from comfortable. Before arriving at Marienbad, ever mindful of courtesies due from one monarch to another, he had enquired whether he might visit the emperor again. Perhaps he was relieved that his request was politely but firmly declined. Sources close to Francis Joseph believed that their master was 'tired of the inward struggle to which personal intercourse with the King had always given rise'.

King Edward VII did not live to see another summer at Marienbad. Spring 1910 was exceptionally cold, and not even his customary holiday in Biarritz could improve his health or spirits. A tendency to bronchitis and anxiety over crises at home and abroad – conflict between the Commons and House of Lords, and the threat of war in Europe which could come at any time – took their toll. Working to the end, as he stubbornly told his doctors he would, on 6 May he retired to bed at Buckingham Palace under protest and died shortly before midnight.

Reaction throughout Europe varied from guarded criticism of 'a mighty and victorious antagonist' in Germany, to genuine sorrow in France, where the prime minister Ribot unequivocally if somewhat prematurely saluted him as 'one of the greatest Kings of England.' The Viennese press regretted with respect the death of 'the most influential man of the present day' who passed away 'at the end of a political era which he, more than any other, had helped to transform'.

Francis Joseph was deeply affected by King Edward's death. His confidantes had never known the demise of a sovereign to have such a profound effect on him. They attributed it either to the fact that he had enjoyed a more lively correspondence with the British king than with any other contemporary monarch, or else to a twinge of conscience at his realisation that he had behaved badly over the annexation crisis. To the end of his life he would talk about the 'true spirit of friendship' in which they had always met.

Even the critical Margutti, who had been deeply suspicious of King Edward, could not completely conceal his admiration. He concluded that the king's attempts to encircle Germany were designed to avert rather than provoke war. German industrial and commercial development, her military and naval expansion, were arousing such a sense of rivalry in England that a crisis was bound to arise – and recourse to arms would be the result:

> King Edward thought such a catastrophe could best be prevented by the complete isolation of Germany, not with a view to aggression against her, but of cooling her ardour for war. I have repeatedly had this view of Edward VII's policy put to me by Englishmen and I really believe this explanation contains a grain of truth.[22]

In Hungary the late king was venerated even more strongly. A memorial service at the Calvintér church, Budapest, was attended by emperor, court, and the cream of Hungarian society. An Anglican vicar paid tribute in his sermon to the sovereign as a lover of peace who had made it the object of his life to use the methods of diplomacy to save Europe from the threat of war. As Margutti left the church afterwards, he was stopped by the minister of defence, Baron von Fejérváry, who remarked to him:

> The English clergyman has taken the words out of my mouth. I – and everyone else who has really considered the question – have

never doubted that Edward VII's whole purpose in pursuing his 'encirclement' policy was to preserve the peace of Europe. The King saw that it was permanently endangered by the antagonism between France and Germany on the one hand and Russia's aspirations in the Balkans on the other hand.

Hence the British alliance with Japan and Edward VII's efforts to keep Germany's military threats within bounds by uniting the rest of Europe against her. It is probable that the future alone will show how far King Edward was right. It is certainly a matter for regret that he is no longer here to preserve that balance which – in his own way, perhaps – he strove so hard to establish.[23]

Fejérváry was not alone in his views. Two other Hungarian ministers, Count Apponyi and Count Andrassy (son of the dual monarchy's first minister of the exterior), had strongly urged a rapprochement between Britain and Austria-Hungary during the annexation crisis.

One year later, the historian Professor Lammasch was still urging this course of action. It was his judgement that a central power occupying such a geographical position as the dual monarchy would inevitably succumb to pressure from all sides, unless a strong foreign power – namely Britain – could use her influence to help protect her from jealous neighbours. To support his theory, he pointed out that every one of Austria-Hungary's neighbours cherished designs on certain parts of her territories, as all of them, especially Germany, had members of their own races within her borders. This did not apply in Britain's case, and as an understanding with the latter would almost certainly lead via the Entente Cordiale to a similar alliance with France, the Habsburg monarchy might look forward to an alliance with two powerful states with which it had no common frontiers.

9.   Crown Prince Rudolf, 1888

10. Queen Victoria and her family at Coburg for the wedding of her grandchildren, Princess Victoria Melita of Saxe-Coburg Gotha and Ernest, Grand Duke of Hesse and the Rhine, April 1894. Seated, left to right: William II, German Emperor; Queen Victoria; Empress Frederick. The standing figures include her three surviving sons, the Prince of Wales (on left) and the Dukes of Connaught and Saxe-Coburg Gotha (on right); Nicholas, Tsarevich of Russia and his fiancee Princess Alix of Hesse; and Count Mensdorff, in silk top hat (centre, back row)

11. King Edward VII and Emperor Francis Joseph at the opera, Vienna, 1 September 1903, after a drawing by Edward Cucuel

12.   Emperor Francis Joseph, from a postcard commemorating his diamond jubilee in 1908

13. King George V, c. 1910

14. Archduke Francis Ferdinand with his wife Sophie, princess of Hohenberg, and their children Ernest, Maximilian and Sophie, 1913

Vier gegen Acht.

Gebt Acht, Ihr „Acht", es blitzt und kracht
und schlägt manch' schwere Lücke.
Jung-Siegfrieds Schwert schlug unversehrt
den Amboß einst in Stücke.
Und Treue, Mut und Einigkeit
Geb' uns zum Siege das Geleit.   Richard Ott.

5377

15.   Contemporary heads of state, from a Great War postcard, c.1915. Top row: Sultan
Mohammed V of Turkey; German Emperor William II with Emperor Francis Joseph;
Ferdinand, Tsar of Bulgaria. Centre row: Nicholas II, Tsar of Russia; King George V;
Raymond Poincare, President of France. The bottom row includes Kings Peter of Serbia,
Victor Emmanuel III of Italy and Albert of Belgium

16. Emperor Charles and Empress Zita at their coronation, Cathedral of Mathias Corvinus, Budapest, 30 December 1916

CHAPTER 8

From Sarajevo to Madeira

The funeral of King Edward VII was held at Windsor on 20 May 1910. Among those who rode in procession behind his successor, King George V, were eight other European crowned heads, five heirs apparent, and a host of princes representing each of the European and several Eastern dynasties. There had never been such a large gathering of monarchs in Britain, not even at Queen Victoria's funeral. Such attendance indicated the immense respect in which King Edward had been held, even by those who regarded him as a dangerous intriguer.

Though King George V as prince of Wales had enjoyed an extraordinarily close relationship with his father, both men differed widely in their attitudes to Europe. King Edward VII loved foreign travel, and had crossed the English channel six times during the last year of his life. His insular son disliked setting foot on the continent, and this aversion increased with age. Abroad, he observed, was 'awful – I know, because I have been there'. He felt more comfortable at home; despite his naval upbringing, his digestion suffered from rough seas and rich, unfamiliar food; and his sketchy education had neglected languages. Even as an adult he could not speak a word of German, and his French was very rudimentary.

Yet at the time of his accession he did not share King Edward's preference for France over Germany. His foreign secretary, Sir Edward Grey, was intent on preserving the Anglo-French entente and thought that the new king's first visit abroad as sovereign should be to Paris. To this King George answered that France was a republic, and the continental monarchies of Austria, Germany and Russia should take preference. Because of Emperor Francis Joseph's advanced age, it was only right that Austria should be given primary consideration. In addition, the king and Mensdorff were on excellent terms. Both men had known each other well for over thirty years, and as a young diplomatic secretary in London Mensdorff had been sufficiently close to the family to be a guest at

Sandringham in January 1892 for the ill-fated duke of Clarence's birthday celebrations. Mensdorff had also caught influenza there but recovered.* King George V wrote regularly to 'My dear Albert' and signed his letters 'Your affectionate friend and cousin.' He assured Mensdorff that Austria enjoyed a special place in the hearts of Englishmen. Yet owing to industrial unrest and the uncertain state of Ulster, there were to be no state visits to imperial Vienna by King George V and Queen Mary.

Archduke Francis Ferdinand was one of the first to send King George a telegram on his accession, and he received a warm reply. They had met on previous occasions – at Vienna in April 1904, and in Madrid two years later, when they were guests at the wedding of King Alfonso XIII of Spain and Princess Victoria Eugenia of Battenberg, an occasion at which all royalties present in the state procession had narrowly missed death from an anarchist bomb. King and archduke had much in common. They were both introverted, happiest in their family and domestic circle, fond of shooting, and interested in the navy. Moreover they came from the same generation, the king being eighteen months younger.

Mindful of these similarities, the archduke lost no time in trying to have Sophie's name included in the royal guest list for King Edward's funeral. Mensdorff gloomily recorded in his diary that he had 'the unhappy idea' of bringing his wife with him, putting her up incognito in a hotel and staying on with him for a few days after the ceremonies were over – still incognito.

Such plans were immediately thwarted by a report in the Vienna papers about the princess of Hohenberg's attendance at the funeral, having apparently been given full permission from the authorities in London. The British embassy in Vienna accordingly notified the foreign office at London, and Mensdorff had the unenviable task of writing to Francis Ferdinand that Her Majesty Queen Mary had already had to refuse the visits of many other princesses close to her. Under the circumstances she had to decline to receive the princess of Hohenberg. Undaunted, the archduke suggested that his wife should arrive at London under 'the strictest possible incognito', under a different name and even at a different time to her husband. When this was rejected, he was furious. By way of compensation, he was accorded first rank after all emperors and kings at the obsequies,

Already angered by this, the occasion was further overshadowed for the Austrian heir by a petty quarrel with Tsar Ferdinand of Bulgaria. The two had travelled together on the Orient express,

* Prince Albert Victor, duke of Clarence and Avondale, was Prince (later King) George's elder brother. A lethargic, dissipated youth with none of George's strength of character, he succumbed to an epidemic of influenza and died six days after his twenty-eighth birthday.

which arrived in Vienna with Ferdinand's private carriage already attached. Francis Ferdinand insisted that his carriage should be placed in front of that of the Bulgarian sovereign, who might be a head of state but of a much newer and less mighty one than the Habsburg empire. The tsar was livid and the archduke smiled to himself until lunchtime, when it dawned on him that he would have to go through the Bulgarian carriage to reach the dining car. He sent a message to the tsar asking if he might proceed through, and was promptly told that he could not. He therefore had to wait, becoming hungrier by the minute, until the train stopped at the next station, and then hurry along the platform to the dining car. After dinner he had to wait again in similar fashion until they reached the next station.

When they arrived at Buckingham Palace along with the other guests, sympathy was overwhelmingly on the archduke's side. Tsar Ferdinand, who had a remarkable talent for making personal enemies, was treated as a virtual outcast for his high-handed behaviour. When the German emperor noticed on one occasion that ex-President Theodore Roosevelt was speaking to him, he interrupted them, turning his back pointedly on Ferdinand, and saying to Roosevelt that he wished to introduce him to King Alfonso of Spain. Turning an angry eye on the tsar, he added, '*He* is worth talking to!'

After these inauspicious overtures, Francis Ferdinand was in a thoroughly unreceptive frame of mind. He found fault with everything and everyone. The funeral ceremony, he insisted, was excessively long. Here he had ample grounds for complaint, for the obsequies lasted from 9 a.m. to 6 p.m. For the last part, in St George's Chapel, there were no chairs provided and the weary guests had to stand. He was less justified in believing that authorities at court had made a disgraceful mistake by fixing the late king's riding boots back to front in the horse's stirrups. This was in fact intentional, for at the funerals of English sovereigns and senior officers, this denoted that their days in the saddle were over.

His official report gave full rein to these complaints and many other trifling errors by the 'arrogant English'. Fortunately his personal attacks stopped short of criticising the king's family, but other guests escaped less lightly. The presidents of France and the United States 'distinguished themselves by an exceptional lack of any courtly manners'. Crown Prince Alexander of Serbia, who was destined to meet his Maker in almost identical fashion to that of the archduke,* looked like 'a bad gypsy'. And Tsar Ferdinand looked 'like a pig' on horseback, a venomous if not altogether inaccurate comparison.

The next link between the courts of Windsor and Vienna came about on a happier occasion, just over a year later – the coronation of King

* See page 146.

George V. By rights, Archduke Francis Ferdinand should have
represented the Habsburgs again, as he had done at King Edward VII's
crowning in 1902, but this time he refused to go in order to spare his
wife another round of petty humiliation.

In his place went Archduke Charles, second in succession to the
imperial throne. Aged twenty-three, Charles was the son of Francis
Ferdinand's younger brother Otto, whose taste for wild living and
escapades of dubious propriety had not been curbed by marriage to
Princess Maria Josepha of Saxony. Nicknamed 'Handsome Otto' by
the Viennese, who looked on him as the perennial playboy of their
ruling dynasty, he died of tuberculosis in 1906.

Much to Emperor Francis Joseph's relief, the shy, affable young
Charles seemed mercifully free of character defects which had plagued
all the other archdukes who had stood in direct line of succession to
the throne. In June 1911 it was announced that he was engaged to be
married to the attractive Princess Zita of Bourbon-Parma. Like that of
Francis Ferdinand and Sophie, this love-match would go against the
Habsburg grain in proving supremely happy; and the harmony of
their married life together would be the only abiding consolation
throughout the rest of Charles's short and troubled life.

The young couple were not allowed long to celebrate their
betrothal. On 17 June, four days after the announcement, Charles left
for London on his first important representative mission abroad.
Delegations from nearly sixty countries descended on the British
capital that week. On 19 June, he was one of twenty-nine princes and
foreign notabilities travelling from Dover to Victoria station in two
special trains. The terminus was carpeted and draped in crimson to
welcome them, and the platform was bedecked with a liberal display
of hydrangeas and carnations.

He and his retinue stayed at 41 Belgrave Square. On his first night
in London, he left for a banquet at Buckingham Palace, followed by a
ball given by the duchess of Sutherland at Staffordshire House, lasting
until the small hours. On coronation day, 22 June, he drove to
Westminster Abbey in a carriage placed just in front of the British
royal family's procession, a distinction shared with the German crown
prince and princess and the crown prince of Egypt.

Charles was much impressed with the dignity and symbolism of the
coronation service. This apart, the event in England which he enjoyed
most was a naval review at Spithead two days later. He always remembered the men-o'-war from all nations lined up offshore, columns of
grey steel by day, turrets of light by night when each lay illuminated
overall on the dark water. Like the coronation, it was a symbol of
British might. At that time, experts maintained that there were sixty-
three British battleships built or under construction, compared with
forty-one belonging to her German rival across the North Sea.

Charles also attended other receptions in which he met the foremost British statesmen of the time, among them Asquith, Haldane, and Grey. Ironically it was the latter who would declare war on Germany and her Austro-Hungarian ally only three years later. These meetings were purely receptions with no aims of political discussion involved, and this suited the young archduke. He had been given no permission to talk about international affairs, and he realised that his sensitive uncle Francis Ferdinand would be watching his movements very carefully.

It did not escape general observation that Charles acted with becoming restraint at the social festivities in London. Though he dutifully stayed till late at all dances to which he was invited, particularly the farewell ball for coronation guests on 28 June given by Lord Derby, he was never seen to dance with anybody. This was regarded as a mark of deep respect to his fiancée, whose portrait he proudly showed to Queen Mary.

Such gestures, and his quiet yet cheerful personality, won him praise from all sides. In Britain the octogenarian emperor, who had never crossed the North Sea, was considered impossibly remote. Crown Prince Rudolf's attendance at the 1887 jubilee celebrations had been speedily eclipsed by the horror of Mayerling. Francis Ferdinand's suspicious, morose personality had done nothing to raise the stock of the Habsburgs in England. It seemed all the more remarkable, therefore, that here was an archduke from the Austrian imperial family against whom nothing could be said.

Archduke Francis Ferdinand's frustration after his attendance at King Edward's funeral soon passed. Mensdorff's conveyance to the archduke of King George V's warmest sympathies had been followed by suggestions that plans might soon be made for the duchess of Hohenberg to accompany her husband to England.

In May 1912 an opportunity presented itself. The English Horticultural Society was about to stage its first international flower show. As the archduke's love of flowers was legendary, and as the rose gardens on his estates at Konopischt were so well-known, he was an obvious guest. Moreover, since he would be coming as a horticulturist and not as the heir to an empire, it was only natural that his wife should be openly included in the invitation. Accordingly, the 'count and countess of Artstetten' journeyed to London together that spring.

During their fortnight in England, the 'count and countess' stayed at the Ritz Hotel in Piccadilly, and visited not only the exhibition (which fascinated them) but also several country houses. Most of these expeditions were arranged by Sophie's niece, Countess Elizabeth Baillet-Latour, then living in England. The most successful was one to Welbeck Abbey, Northamptonshire, where the duke of Portland bade them return for shooting the following autumn.

Most important of all, Mensdorff arranged their first welcome at the court of St James. On 23 May, Francis Ferdinand and Sophie sat down to lunch at Buckingham Palace with King George V, Queen Mary, and Dowager Queen Alexandra. Their guests, the king noted afterwards, were 'charming and made themselves very pleasant'. Like many shy people of noble blood, the archduke often gave the appearance of being anything but charming in public, but on private occasions – as indeed in his own domestic circle – he was a model of civility and kindness.

Even better was to come. When Mensdorff mentioned the Welbeck invitation to King George in July 1913, the king suggested that the Austrian heir and his wife should combine this with a visit to Windsor for another week's shooting that same season. The archduke accepted most fulsomely, asking Mensdorff to tell His Majesty how 'quite exceptionally enchanted' he and the duchess felt at the prospect. It did not matter that their sojourn would be a private affair; on the contrary, he looked forward to avoiding 'terrible banquets and toasts'. The equally retiring king would not have been out of sympathy with such sentiments.

Despite his request for formalities to be kept to a minimum, Francis Ferdinand and Sophie were honoured on the weekend of their arrival in November 1913 with a dinner party at the embassy in London. This represented a considerable step forward, for it was now acknowledged that there was no need for incognita. The princess of Hohenberg may not have been an archduchess, but she was being granted full honours due to a future empress–consort. On the following Monday they all went by train to Windsor, where King George was awaiting them on the platform. Malicious tongues commented on Queen Mary's absence, but no slight was intended as it was her customary practice to await royal guests, other than crowned heads, at the castle.

At Windsor king and archduke made the most of the shooting, though there was a political twist to the conversation when guests such as Grey and Lord Rosebery joined them. But the main aim of the excursion, from Francis Ferdinand's point of view, was to set the British seal of approval on Sophie's equal rights; his wishes could not have been fulfilled more adequately.

Yet they had both been a little in awe of their hosts at Windsor. During their subsequent stay at Welbeck, they could relax more. Archduke and the duke of Portland were already close friends, and as the duchess had been born a mere Miss Dallas-Yorke, Sophie could feel at ease and need have no fears about their hosts' aristocratic superiority.

Successful as the shooting was, the party had one alarming moment. There was thick snow on the ground at Welbeck, and while they were out one of the loaders tripped, accidentally discharging both barrels of his gun. The shots went within a few feet of the archduke. In later years the duke of Portland was often moved to wonder whether the great war might have been averted or delayed if the archduke had met an untimely death there and then. Far from being angry, Francis Ferdinand was in such a genial frame of mind that he dismissed his narrow escape as a natural sporting hazard.

As the happy days in England were drawing to a close, Queen Mary could not be more fulsome about her husband's guests. On 27 November she wrote to her aunt Augusta, duchess of Mecklenburg-Strelitz:

> The Archduke was formerly very anti-English but that is quite changed now, and her influence has been and is good, they say, in every way. All the people staying with us who had known him before said how much he had changed for the better and that he was most enthusiastic over his visit to us and to England. . .[1]

Much was read into the political implications of this visit. As it was private, the assertions of Francis Ferdinand's secretary that he sought to play the role of mediator between the mutually suspicious England and Germany were undoubtedly exaggerated.

Yet Archduchess Zita, who saw much of her uncle at this time, was certain that he wanted a revival of the 'Three Emperors League' between Germany, Austria and Russia, and as an additional safeguard sought 'the greatest possible participation of England' in this new alignment of the powers. While King Edward VII was on the throne, personal antagonism between him and Emperor William II made such a possibility remote. With King George V, a model constitutional monarch who never aspired to emulate his father's diplomatic role, it was surely feasible. Francis Ferdinand was uniquely placed to bring such a move about. As they happily celebrated Christmas 1913 with their children, Francis Ferdinand and Sophie had much to be contented about. Far from begrudging them their success, Emperor Francis Joseph unbent sufficiently at the Vienna court ball of February 1914 – the last, as it turned out – to ask Sophie spontaneously to come and sit next to him.

In March 1914 the Portlands accepted a return invitation to Konopischt. While they were there, they discussed the idea of King George and Queen Mary coming to stay at the archducal autumn retreat, Bluhnbach, in September. Later there was talk of this visit being combined with that of Emperor William at Konopischt for the autumn shooting. What could not be achieved informally through a friendly meeting between the English and German sovereigns on Austrian territory? Emperor Francis Joseph had again fallen foul of his regular enemy, bronchitis, that spring, and at the age of eighty-three he was unlikely to last much longer. By September, it might well be the case that King George and Emperor William would be welcomed by Emperor Francis Ferdinand – with perhaps Empress Sophie by his side.

At last, it seemed that a genuine bond was forming between the courts of St James and Vienna. The link between Albert Edward, prince of Wales, and Crown Prince Rudolf, had been social rather than political. Both being heirs, not crowned heads, prevented any close connections of state authority. Now, a firmer association uniting the ruling houses and their courts seemed well within grasp.

It was Europe's tragedy that fate decreed otherwise.

1913 was the last year of the old European order. In the phrase of Virginia Cowles, it was 'the defiant swansong'; according to Winston Churchill, 'the vials of wrath were full'.

Royalties flocked to Berlin in May for the wedding of Emperor William's only daughter, Victoria Louise, to the duke of Brunswick. Superficially, the welcome given by William to his cousins King George V and Tsar Nicholas II of Russia was warm enough, though George suspected that their host's ear was glued to the keyhole every time he and 'cousin Nicky' attempted to have a private conversation. Nobody – least of all the crowned heads themselves – could yet see that the destiny of mutually-suspicious nations had passed from the control of their rulers to military commanders – the 'dreadful militarism' of which the far-sighted Empress Frederick had written and warned so prophetically. In Russia, while the court celebrated the Romanovs' tercentenary as a ruling dynasty, Lenin was writing hopefully to Maxim Gorky that 'a war with Austria would be a splendid little thing for the revolution' if only the emperors would be so obliging.

Already Francis Ferdinand, newly appointed general inspector of the Austro-Hungarian military forces, was a marked man. Serbia's dreams of expansion and liberation had been growing steadily since the ill-considered annexation of Bosnia and Herzegovina. Statesmen and terrorist organisations in the country may have been impatient of each others' methods, but they shared the same objective – to achieve unity for all Serbs, including those who still lived under Turkish and Hungarian rule, and particularly those in Bosnia under Austrian rule.

Of the undercover groups in Serbia, the most notorious was that known as the 'Black Hand'. Francis Ferdinand had been made aware of its existence through his private military and intelligence staff, and it was probable that he knew its ringleaders were after his blood. His plan to bring together Austria's Serbo-Croat citizens and grant them equality with other national groups living within the Austro-Hungarian empire ran counter to their aims for Serbia's future.

Events at the Bosnian capital Sarajevo in June 1914, and the months of preparation for that catastrophic journey, have been documented in minute detail elsewhere. In brief, the idea of Archduke Francis Ferdinand going to the town on a military tour of inspection during the summer of 1914 was widely known the previous winter, and members of the Black Hand urged all patriotic Serbs to take 'holy vengeance' on the Habsburg dynasty. He was warned that his life would probably be threatened if he went, but he was no coward. 'It is my duty,' he insisted. When consulted, Francis Joseph sent word that his heir was to do as he wished. It was the archduke's deliberate intention to take Sophie, for after their triumphant reception in England, there would be no official objection to her riding with him in a stately procession where she could receive the full honours due to her as the wife of the next emperor.

In April, the emperor's health gave cause for anxiety. His bronchial attacks became so severe, and medical bulletins were worded so cautiously, that in Belgrade the conspirators whispered among themselves that their weapons would not be needed after all. If Emperor Francis Joseph was so ill, his heir would not be coming to Bosnia that summer. Not until the end of May was he pronounced out of danger. Had he not recovered, the lives of his heir and consort would have been spared – and many other lives in the next four years as well. Rarely can the progress of a monarch's illness have had such a fateful bearing on the destiny of a continent.

On 28 June, Francis Ferdinand and Sophie took their places in the motorcade through the streets of Sarajevo to inspect the forces, visit the main hall for a reception, and go to see a folk museum. The morning, a day of blazing sunshine with no breeze to give them respite from the heat, was one of several anniversaries. It was the fourteenth wedding anniversary of the august couple; the anniversary of the battle at Kossovo in 1389 at which the Turks had destroyed medieval Serbia, a day of national mourning and vengeance; and, more recently, the first anniversary of vengeance fulfilled, namely Serbian victory in the second Balkan war.

About ten minutes after the motorcade had entered the city, a bomb was thrown at the car. It passed behind Sophie, who was grazed slightly by the fuse cap – and severely shaken. The car behind them was wrecked; the occupants and several onlookers were injured, though none fatally. Francis Ferdinand arrived at the city hall angry and unnerved after their narrow escape, but having vented his fury on the unfortunate mayor he regained his composure.

After listening to the mayor's speech and replying with a stiffly-worded message of thanks, the archduke enquired after those who had been wounded, with a view to visiting them in hospital. There was confusion about the rest of the day's itinerary; should the museum trip be deferred, or should the complete programme be cancelled? The processional route was altered at such short notice that nobody thought to inform the driver of the leading car. At a crucial turning, the chauffeur was ordered to change his route.

As he stopped to reverse and the cars came to a halt, a youth named Gavrilo Princip stood on the corner watching. A member of the Black Hand, Princip had been thrown into a panic by the failure of the would-be assassin, Nedjelko Cabrinovic, and feared that he would be seized for questioning because of his complicity. Now, without warning, he found the Habsburg target and his wife within about ten feet of him. Drawing a loaded pistol from his pocket, he stepped into the street and fired twice; the police reached him just as he was about to try and turn the gun on himself.

As the chauffeur turned the second car around, Sophie collapsed against her husband; she had died almost instantaneously. He made a valiant effort to prevent her from falling, entreating her to live for the sake of their children. Muttering, 'It is nothing,' feebly over and over again, he slumped forward and expired just as the cars were reaching the governor's residence.

Several European crowned heads, consorts or their heirs had fallen victim to assassins within the preceding four decades – Tsar Alexander II of Russia in 1881; Empress Elizabeth in 1898; King Humbert of Italy in 1900; King Carlos of Portugal and his heir the duke of Braganza in 1908; and King George of Greece in 1913. Only eleven years earlier, King Alexander and Queen Draga of Serbia had been butchered in a palace revolution at Belgrade with several of their relations, servants and ministers, on a night of violence which had sent a shudder through the continent.* The events at Sarajevo, therefore, appeared at first no more than just another grim reminder of royal and imperial mortality. Though the news had reached Vienna and her newspapers by mid-afternoon, no mood of mourning was discernible among the crowds enjoying the midsummer sunshine.

'Terrible shock for the dear old Emperor,'[2] King George V noted in his diary. Francis Ferdinand and Sophie had been his guests so recently, and he and Queen Mary had found them such excellent company, that he really felt as though he had lost two good friends. A court ball planned at Buckingham Palace for Monday 29 June was cancelled, and one week's mourning was proclaimed. In defiance of protocol, he made an informal visit to Mensdorff at the Austrian embassy to express his dismay at the outrage. Neither King George

---

* The Serbs had subsequently invited Prince Peter Karageorgevic to assume the crown. In June 1914 he appointed his son Crown Prince Alexander (the 'bad gypsy' at King Edward VII's funeral) to act as regent. It was rumoured that Alexander was privy to the assassination plot. Ironically he too was murdered on an official visit abroad. Succeeding his father as king of Serbia and then Yugoslavia in 1921, he was shot in Marseilles by a Croatian terrorist in October 1934, shortly after beginning a state visit to France.

nor his government realised its significance for a while, though many an European embassy knew otherwise. While the late archduke's contemptuous verdict on Serbia as a country of 'rascals, fools and prune trees' might have been widely shared by his fellow-Austrians, Sir Arthur Nicolson, a former British ambassador in Vienna, forecast gloomily that the Balkan kingdom could one day set Europe by the ears and bring about a universal war on the continent.

On 30 June, at question time in the house of commons, Asquith formally expressed parliament's 'indignation and deep concern' at the assassinations, and profound sympathy with the imperial family, at 'one of those incredible crimes which almost makes us despair of the progress of mankind'. With that, Westminster turned her attention to what appeared an infinitely more pressing problem, that of unrest in Ulster. Meanwhile, it was announced that Prince Arthur of Connaught would represent his cousin King George V at the archduke's funeral.*

'I am spared nothing,' Francis Joseph sobbed to his new heir Charles, equally shocked himself. 'But at least I can rely on you.'

As the historian H.A.L. Fisher observed some twenty years later, 'it was as if, at a moment of acute political tension, the Prince of Wales had been murdered in Ireland'.[3] Throughout Austria-Hungary it was assumed, if not actually believed, that the Habsburg heir's assassination had been prompted or connived at by members of the Serbian government. An inquiry by Austrian agents found no direct evidence of official Serbian complicity, but justice had to be done. On 23 July an ultimatum was sent from Vienna to Serbia. Sir Edward Grey later commented that he had never seen one nation address to another independent state a document of so formidable a character. Serbia was prepared to accept some but not all of its demands, and the labyrinth of alliances between one country and another slowly but inexorably ground into action. Russia, champion of the Slavs, took the side of Serbia; Germany, faithful to her obligations, stood by Austria. On 1 August she declared war on Russia, and on 3 August on France and Belgium. On 4 August Britain declared war on Germany; on 5 August Austria declared war on Russia; on 12 August Britain was at war with Austria.

That day Mensdorff received a kindly letter from King George V, referring to their old friendship and lifelong intimacy, and hoping to welcome him back to London one day. It was surely without precedent in history, he thought, that the sovereign could write such a warmly personal letter to the ambassador of an enemy power on the declaration of war between both, that ended 'ever your devoted

---

* European courts were informed soon afterwards that the presence of their delegates at the funeral was not required, in order to spare the aged emperor the strain of entertaining guests.

friends and cousins'.[4] A much-repeated joke of the day attributed the delay in Britain's declaration of war on the Habsburg empire as deliberate, so as to allow Mensdorff time to complete his programme of country-house visits first.

Austria shared no part of the bitter resentment which Britain felt for Germany as a nation and for Germans as individuals. Lord Harewood, whose son later married Mary, Princess Royal, wrote to Mensdorff (14 August) how lamentable it was that their nations should be at war, 'for we owe you no grudge except for having put the match to the fire.'[5]*

The old order throughout Europe had signed its death warrant. A war which was confidently expected by many of the military commanders, particularly in Germany, to be over by Christmas 1914, dragged on four long years. By the time the defeated nations had laid down their arms, nearly nine million men had perished in combat; nearly twenty-one million were wounded; and hunger and disease, notably a savage epidemic of Spanish influenza, also exacted its vicious toll on a weary continent.

After sixty-five years on the throne, Francis Joseph was exhausted, too bowed down by the burdens of empire and old age to realise that the vendetta he wished to pursue against Serbia for reasons of national prestige would engulf the whole of Europe. The ostensibly gentle octogenarian of imperial Vienna was almost as responsible for the outbreak of hostilities as his more conspicuous ally, the *pickelhaube*-clad *enfant terrible* in Berlin. Though he had no quarrel with Britain or France, his blind allegiance to Germany had placed the Austrian emperor at odds with these once-friendly powers.

There were times when he appeared to acknowledge this with the deepest regret, and lament the death of King Edward VII, perhaps the only sovereign upon whom he could have relied implicitly. To confidantes, he remarked sadly that 'with genius like his he'd never have let this terrible war break out. . .He ought to have lived a little longer to control this awful situation. I realise more and more every day that he is no longer with us.'[6]

But even in his dotage, the emperor was as chivalrous as ever. Keenly aware of the privilege of his appointment in 1896 as colonel-

---

* Despite rumours in the press that he was said to have spoken insultingly about Britain during the war, the royal hand of friendship was extended again to Mensdorff in peacetime. From 1927 onwards he was an annual guest at Sandringham, and once again he was asked to wear his insignia of the Royal Victorian Order. In November 1935 he remarked to a friend that 'When the King is standing he reminds me of the Emperor Francis Joseph in his last years.' Two months later King George V passed away peacefully in his seventy-first year. Mensdorff, like the venerable emperor, lived to a ripe old age; he died in 1945, aged eighty-four.

in-chief of the 1st Queen's (now King's) Dragoon Guards, he wrote to the regiment shortly after declaration of war. He had given orders to his troops, he said, that should any officer or soldier of the guards be so unfortunate as to be taken prisoner, he was to be regarded as a personal guest of the emperor for the duration of hostilities.[7]

Too old and frail to do much more than study the documents submitted to him merely to occupy his time, the emperor lived out his last two years virtually a prisoner at Schönbrunn. Part of the park adjacent to the palace was closed to the public, who thus no longer saw him. It was rumoured that he had died and his death was being kept secret for patriotic reasons. Grieved by Austrian military reverses, and yet another assassination – this time no relation, but instead his chief minister Count Karl Sturgkh – he fell prey to his old adversary bronchitis. To the very end of his life he rose early and worked diligently at his desk, signing endless papers which his weak eyes could barely see and his tired mind hardly understand.

He still remained a tool of the Habsburg protocol which had governed almost very moment of every day. The story is often told that one night he was awoken by a severe fit of choking. He rang for his personal physician, who felt that in an emergency etiquette must take second place to medical necessity. Donning a dressing gown and seizing his bag of medicines, he hurried through the palace to his master's bedroom. At the sight of such undignified garb, Francis Joseph sat up angrily in bed and croaked, '*Frach!*' ('Frock-coat!') The doctor's slovenly dress, it seems, cured him on this occasion.

On 20 November 1916, the feverish emperor was working at his desk as usual. After the documents were signed, his attendant suggested that 'Your Majesty should rest now' – something no servant would have dared to say under normal circumstances. With a gentle smile, the monarch replied that he would be resting soon enough. Next day he was helped to his bed in a state of collapse. Slipping in and out of consciousness several times, he died shortly after nine in the evening. He was eighty-six years of age. Had he lived another eleven days, he would have completed a reign of sixty-eight years. Already he had surpassed Queen Victoria's record (sixty-three years) as the longest-reigning European monarch since King Louis XIV, of France, who had worn his crown for almost seventy-two.

Two days later King George V noted in his diary that the late emperor 'indeed had an unhappy and stormy life'.[8] *The Times* was more expansive:

> The death of the Austrian Emperor removes a figure that seemed to have become a permanent figure of the political configuration of Europe. For more than threescore years he had stood erect while others came and went. . . Neither Maria Theresa, with

whom Francis Joseph will rank in Habsburg annals, nor Louis XIV, nor Queen Victoria, who alone surpassed or rivalled him in length of reign, were exposed to vicissitudes such as taxed his pliancy and tried his fortitude.[9]

Already the paper recognised that it was unquestionable Austria did the bidding of Berlin:

The direct responsibility of Francis Joseph for this criminal policy cannot be ascertained. Age probably rendered him incapable of resisting pressure which in earlier years he might have had the strength to withstand. Rather than upon him, responsibility falls upon the German Emperor, the German military party, and their accomplices in Austria, and particularly in Hungary. . .When he is borne to his last resting place in the Capuchin vault, the world will reflect that an era which might have been a great era in Habsburg history has closed amid ruin, bankruptcy, blood and tears; but in these reflections there will be place for human compassion with the lot of a man who came as a stripling to the throne, who saw brother, wife, son and nephew perish by 'violence, who lost the fairest provinces of his empire, and who must have ended a long and chequered reign with forebodings of disaster to his House and his dominions graver than any which even he had known.[10]

At the age of twenty-nine, Charles was emperor of Austria-Hungary. 'There is no reason to suppose that the young ruler will rise in character or in statecraft above the somewhat low average of Habsburg rulers',[11] *The Times* wrote rather unkindly. What it omitted to mention was the magnitude of the task which faced Francis Joseph's successor – to avert in any way possible the impending collapse of a disintegrating empire whose decay had been self-evident even before it was precipitated into war. Totally opposed to the horrors of battle, Charles's overriding intention was to win back for his subjects 'the sorely-missed blessings of peace'.

Though he valued good relations with Germany, he recognised that his great-uncle's stubborn allegiance to the time-honoured alliance between both empires had been a grave error, although he bore no animosity against Emperor William. On the contrary, he regarded him with considerable respect and sympathy, realising as a fellow head of state that William was dominated by the Prussian military establishment, and committed against his better judgement to the almost hopeless cause of total victory at any cost.

In 1917 the Romanovs were overthrown by the Bolshevik revolution, an upheaval which took Russia out of the war. Though this removed an enemy from Austria's eastern front, prospects were still ominous for the Austro-Hungarian empire. The doomed Italian campaign was a heavy drain on resources, and to make matters worse the United States of America entered the war on the allied side. The German high command did nothing to hide its view that Austria was a vastly inferior ally, if not a burden.

Charles, backed strongly by Empress Zita, felt that the only course of action was to sue for a separate peace. Britain and France were only theoretically at war with Austria-Hungary, and their forces never clashed except for occasional naval encounters in the Adriatic Sea. The only allied power seriously engaged against the dual monarchy was Italy.

As an intermediary between the Allied and Entente powers, Charles chose his brother-in-law Prince Sixtus of Bourbon-Parma. Both men, as well as the empress, saw a brighter chance for Europe with a separate negotiated peace, followed by an alliance between Austria, Britain and France. Sixtus went on a peace mission to President Poincaré of France, and the latter undertook to write to King George V and his prime minister David Lloyd George.

Arrangements were made for ministerial visits to England in order to further the plan. Unfortunately for all concerned, a change of administration in France soon followed. The cabinet of Aristide Briand, a strong supporter of Austria and the Habsburg dynasty, was replaced by a government headed by Alexandre Ribot, who had no such enthusiasm for these proposals.

Yet Ribot was obliged to pursue his predecessor's mission. In April he sailed to Folkestone for a secret discussion with Lloyd George, taking a letter from Emperor Charles. After lengthy talks, they reluctantly came to the conclusion that no immediate response to Vienna was possible. Italy would have to be consulted first, and as the Italians had been brought into the war almost wholly with promises of territorial gains at Austria's expense, the plan seemed doomed.

But Charles was encouraged by this initial Anglo-French enthusiasm. In May he wrote Sixtus a second letter which, while recognising opposition to any form of peace in which Italy did not participate, held out hopes for an Italian peace overture in which she was prepared to compromise on her annexation demands. The understanding which had been reached in Austria-Hungary with France and England on many essential points 'will enable us, we feel sure, to overcome whatever obstacles may remain in the way of an honourable peace'.[12]

From this point, Ribot perceptibly lost enthusiasm, and Lloyd George became the driving force, pursuing peace initiatives with characteristic zeal, urging Britain's allies and his own sovereign that the sooner the Austrian emperor's offers for an end to conflict were taken up, the better it would be for Europe. Any Italian obstacles must be surmounted, not used as an excuse to dismiss the idea. While Prince Sixtus left Paris for London with the impression that Poincaré was 'very quick-witted and clear-sighted', Lloyd George was described with admiration by the French foreign office as 'an impetuous Celt'.

No sooner had prince and British prime minister met on 23 May 1917 at 10 Downing Street, than the latter was describing Charles's letter as 'very kind', and discussing a meeting with heads of state. Lloyd George wanted no diplomats, he said derisively; they 'were invented to waste time'. Almost immediately he was telephoning King George V to ask for an audience, which took place later that day at Buckingham Palace. No account of the meeting survives, apart from a brief reference in King George's diary, where he mentioned that the concept of separate peace with the Entente was still very secret, and Italy was 'the difficulty'. But 'it would be a great thing if it could be brought about'.[13]

Italy was not the major difficulty. Such a dubious honour went to Germany, or more specifically the faith of General Ludendorff and his military staff in eventual German victory. Count Ottokar Czernin, Austrian minister of the exterior, was so under German influence that he believed any separate Austrian peace would be tantamount to betrayal of their ally.

It was with a heavy heart that King George wrote to Lloyd George on Christmas Day 1917 of his fears that it would be impossible to get Austria to make a separate peace 'as at present she is entirely in the hands of Germany'. Lloyd George himself held out little hope, but still pledged his support for a revitalised Austria in which she could become a thoroughly liberal empire, having much the same relationship with central Europe as Britain had with her scattered dominions around the globe. She would therefore have 'a mission in the future even greater than her mission in the past'. If the peace initiative could be carried through against lengthening odds, this might be achieved under Charles, who was obviously an intelligent young monarch with progressive ideas, anxiously awaiting an opportunity to put them into practice.

It was not to be. In October 1918 the German and Austrian forces went down together. Too late Charles renounced the German alliance and signed an armistice with Britain and France on 4 November. Time was running out for both empires; in Vienna (as in Berlin) revolutionary crowds demanded a republic, and on 9 November Charles was presented with a document of abdication. He had no choice but to sign.

Technically the document was a manifesto agreed jointly by members of the last imperial cabinet and socialist ministers of the new republic. As far as the emperor was concerned, it required him to recognise in advance any new constitution that might be decided upon, and to relinquish all participation in affairs of state. In other words, the last ruler of the Habsburg dynasty was to renounce his power but not his crown.

That evening Charles decided to leave Schönbrunn with his family for safety. He chose Eckartsau, north-east of Vienna, where he had a hunting lodge which was his own private property and not a state dwelling. By Christmas, however, pressure was already being exerted on him to leave Austria or to renounce the crown. Hearing of his uncomfortable position and ill-health (he suffered from heart trouble, and influenza soon after departure from Vienna had weakened him further), King George became concerned for his safety.

Early in February 1919 Prince Sixtus approached Poincaré in Paris. He was anxious that, if the revolutionary government in Austria should fall into the hands of the extreme left, there might be a repetition of events in Russia where ex-Tsar Nicholas and his family had been savagely butchered by the Bolsheviks. Poincaré replied sadly that he had little freedom of action, but agreed with Sixtus that he should consult King George.

On his arrival in London, Sixtus called on the foreign office, and then at Buckingham Palace, where he was received by the king in the presence of Queen Mary. He described to them the tense situation in Austria, and the dangers faced by the emperor and his family. Then he referred to the Romanov tragedy, saying that a repetition of this was possible. He realised that this would strike a chord with the king, who continually reproached himself for the fate which had overtaken his gentle cousins Nicholas and Alexandra and their children, after a plan to send a British cruiser to bring them to safety in Britain had been cancelled.

Profoundly moved, Queen Mary turned to her husband and remarked how serious matters were, whereupon the king promised to do what was possible. Stressing that the need for military protection above all was urgent, and adding that France was certain to give at least diplomatic support, Sixtus bowed and took his leave.

One week later, Charles and Zita were informed that a British officer was being attached to the imperial family for their protection. The officer chosen was Colonel Summerhayes of the royal army medical corps; he had been evacuating prisoners of war in Germany and Austria, and accepted the task enthusiastically. On 21 February the emperor wrote to thank King George for his courteous action, praising the colonel for his charm and tact in such a difficult situation for them all.

However, he was not to stay with them long. The war office at Whitehall considered that, in sending out one of their representatives, they ran the risk of being politically implicated, with possibly detrimental results for British relations with the Austrian republic.

A decision was made to replace him with Lieutenant-Colonel Edward Strutt, a Catholic with a distinguished war record whose skills included a fluent command of German. Strutt became deeply devoted to his charges, accompanying Charles on long walks in the woods around Eckartsau. Among other topics of conversation the emperor talked about his reliance on King George, saying that he trusted him more implicitly than any other crowned head. He informed Strutt that the escutcheons of distinguished British people still hung in the Stefanskirche, and was curious to know whether His Majesty had retained the Austrian banners at St George's Chapel, Windsor.

But Charles could not leave his inheritance in limbo indefinitely. He was aware that monarchist sentiment was still widespread throughout Austria, and at thirty-one he was still young enough to hope that he could resume his position as head of state before long. Moreover he felt some responsibility for trying to save his empire from the red menace.

In March he sent a letter by courier to King Alfonso of Spain, as a head of state which had been neutral during the war and an intermediary in the abortive peace negotiations with President Wilson of the United States. In it he asked Alfonso to pass on to the Entente governments a stern warning that Bolshevism might devour all constituent states of the old empire unless they took swift action to prevent it. He suggested the despatch of Entente troops into the Danube area specifically to keep radicalism under control; delivery of as much food as possible to prevent unrest resulting from famine; and Entente support for a confederation to be reformed from the nations of the old empire under Habsburg leadership.

With what appeared to be fortuitous timing, King Alfonso received the letter just after a communist coup in Budapest. He passed the message on as requested to King George among others. The latter, concerned as he was at the danger, could do no more than acknowledge it and say that a translation of Charles's letter had been passed to the prime minister for discussion at the forthcoming peace conference.

Although the Entente powers were all alarmed at the threat of a possible Bolshevik takeover in their lands, they had scant enthusiasm for the idea of a revived Habsburg confederation. The contents of the letter were kept secret, but it was only to be expected that the Austrians (like the French and Portuguese in recent years) would gradually accustom themselves to republicanism.

While Charles, Alfonso and George were engaged in their three-way correspondence, the republic's first parliament was assembling in Vienna. One of the government's priorities was to resolve decisively the position of its former sovereign. It confronted him with three alternatives. If the emperor and empress would abdicate all rights they could live in Austria as private citizens; if the emperor refused to abdicate he must be exiled; if he refused to abdicate and leave, he would be interned.

On 17 March, Strutt received a personal telegram from the war office at Whitehall, telling him that it was 'highly advisable to get the Emperor out of Austria and into Switzerland at once', adding rather strangely that the British government could not guarantee them a safe journey. Gently he broke the news to Charles and persuaded him and Zita that it was vital for them to move. At length they agreed, on condition that he (Strutt) would understand that their departure was in no sense abdication from the throne.

To mark his exile from Austrian soil, Charles signed a document known to posterity as the 'Feldkirch manifesto'. This was designed to demonstrate to his people and to the world that their emperor had merely undertaken an act of voluntary self-banishment, and to declare the new republican government 'null and void' for him and his house. It was a symbolic if pathetic gesture to maintain the pride of the Habsburgs and not to admit defeat. Yet Charles was not too proud to remember the monarch who, more than any other, helped him and his family safely into exile. Soon after settling in Switzerland, he wrote to King George V, thanking him once again for his generosity and concern.

Charles, Zita and their five children moved first to Chateau Wartegg, close to the Austrian border; later, partly for political reasons and partly owing to shortage of space, they moved to the more roomy Villa Prangins on Lake Geneva. Here their sixth child, a boy christened Rudolf, was born in May 1919.

In March 1921 Charles slipped across the border into Austria with his passport, disguised as a Portuguese gardener from the villa. From there he smuggled himself into Hungary, convinced of the loyalty of his people and trusting in the promises of Admiral Horthy, who had acted as regent since the declaration of a republic, and had vowed to assist him in regaining his throne. But Horthy had become too fond of power to relinquish his position, and insisted that Charles must leave Hungarian soil. On his return to Switzerland, the government proved less accommodating than formerly, and requested the family to leave their territory by January 1922.

They were still looking for another place of asylum when Charles was persuaded to attempt a coup. They flew into Hungary on a plane piloted by two loyal Hungarian airmen on 20 October, and marched on Budapest with a faithful monarchist army behind them. For a while fortune seemed to be favouring the Habsburgs. Not until a skirmish in the city suburbs on 23 October did a combination of last-minute luck on the republican side and treachery among Charles's 'supporters' save Admiral Horthy's position. Sadly, Charles conceded defeat and ordered his forces to surrender.

On 24 October, the French prime minister Briand formally disassociated himself from the former sovereign whom his country had secretly supported for so long. He called upon the Hungarian government to proclaim the deposition of King Charles and hand him over to the British naval Danube flotilla presently in Budapest. From there, he would be conducted to the Black Sea and put on board a British cruiser.

A suggestion was made that Malta might become a temporary home for Charles and his family, but this was ruled out as the prince of Wales was due to visit the island shortly. To have the Habsburgs in residence would be inconvenient and politically insensitive. The peace conference contemplated having them interned in a British possession, but the majority present 'were opposed to Great Britain being his gaoler'. Instead the island of Madeira was chosen, and Charles and Zita were conveyed on the British monitor *Glow-Worm*. They landed at Funchal on 19 November.

The remaining weeks of the year 1921 were taken up with arguments around Europe as to who should be responsible for maintaining this almost penniless family. The great powers were anxious to prevent any money reaching them from private sources, fearful that it might provide Charles with the wherewithal to escape from the island (as Napoleon had done from Elba just over a century earlier) and take advantage of monarchical sentiment to set the war-weary continent in turmoil once again.

They need not have been so concerned. Charles had never been strong, and the misfortunes that had befallen him with merciless regularity since his accession to the throne in November 1916 had taken their toll of the sorely-tried young monarch. Chilly weather and a chronic shortage of money which denied them their fair share of material comforts, including medical attention, did the rest.

In March 1922 a severe cold developed into bronchitis. By the time he felt his illness was bad enough to throw economy to the winds and allow a doctor to be summoned, one of his lungs was already affected. Prematurely aged beyond his thirty-four years, he died on 1 April 1922. Yet despite a life dogged with disaster, he had been granted one privilege denied the Emperor Francis Joseph and his heirs who had predeceased him. Charles was unique in that he died in his bed, surrounded to the end by a devoted wife and children.

'A pathetic figure disappears from the world,' was the verdict of *The Times*. 'More sinned against than sinning, the victim of circumstances he had not created and was powerless to contend against, he deserved pity rather than censure.'[14]

Chronology

1848   'Year of revolutions'; abdication of Emperor Ferdinand and accession of Francis Joseph
1850   Visit of General Haynau to England
1851   Great Exhibition, London; visit of Lajos Kossuth to England; resignation of Lord Palmerston as foreign secretary
1853   Attempted assassination of Francis Joseph
1854   Great Britain and France declare war on Russia; marriage of Francis Joseph and Elizabeth of Bavaria
1855   Death of Tsar Nicholas I of Russia and accession of Alexander II; birth of Sophie, first child of Francis Joseph; appointment of Lord Palmerston as prime minister
1856   Treaty of Paris ends Crimean war; birth of Gisela
1857   First joint visit of Francis Joseph and Elizabeth to Hungary, cut short by death of Sophie; visit of Maximilian and Charlotte to England, followed by their marriage
1858   Birth of Rudolf
1859   Austro-Italian war, battles of Magenta and Solferino, and treaty of Villafranca
1860   Elizabeth's flight to Madeira
1861   Elizabeth's return to Vienna and flight to Corfu; death of prince consort
1862   First visit of prince of Wales to Vienna; Bismarck appointed minister-president of Prussia
1863   First meeting of Queen Victoria and Emperor Francis Joseph; Maximilian formally offered crown of Mexico and requested to renounce rights to Austrian succession
1864   Prusso-Danish war over duchies of Schleswig and Holstein, concluded by treaty of Vienna; Maximilian and Carlota proclaimed emperor and empress of Mexico
1865   Convention of Gastein
1866   Six weeks' war between Austria and Prussia, battle of Königgrätz, and treaty of Prague; dissolution of German confederation; return of Carlota to Europe
1867   *Ausgleich*, or rapprochement with Hungary, and coronation of Francis Joseph and Elizabeth as king and queen; execution of Maximilian at Queretaro; International Exhibition, Paris

1868   Birth of Valerie
1869   First joint visit of prince and princess of Wales to Vienna
1870   France declares war on Prussia, followed by French defeat and abdication of Napoleon III
1871   Proclamation of French republic and German empire; peace signed at treaty of Frankfurt
1872   Death of Sophie, mother of Francis Joseph
1873   International exhibition, Vienna, visited by prince of Wales and Prince Arthur; marriage of Gisela and Leopold of Bavaria
1874   First visit of Elizabeth to Isle of Wight
1875   Death of ex-Emperor Ferdinand
1876   First visit of Elizabeth to mainland Britain for hunting season
1877   Russia declares war on Turkey
1878   First visit of Rudolf to Britain; Russo–Turkish war concluded by treaty of San Stefano, followed by congress of Berlin; Austria given mandate to occupy Bosnia and Herzegovina; death of Francis Charles, father of Francis Joseph
1879   First visit of Elizabeth to Ireland for hunting; dual alliance signed by Austria and Germany, to last till 1884 but continues to 1918
1880   Second visit of Elizabeth to Ireland for hunting
1881   Assassination of Tsar Alexander II of Russia and accession of Alexander III; marriage of Rudolf and Stephanie
1882   Triple alliance, secret treaty between Germany, Austria and Italy, signed and thence renewed regularly until 1915
1883   Birth of Elizabeth, only child of Rudolf
1885   Beginning of friendship between Francis Joseph and Katherine Schratt
1887   Queen Victoria's jubilee, attended by Rudolf among others; probable start of Rudolf's infatuation with Marie Vetsera
1888   Deaths of German Emperors William I and Frederick III, and accession of William II; second meeting of Queen Victoria and Francis Joseph; 'Vienna Incident' involving William II and prince of Wales
1889   Deaths of Rudolf and Marie Vetsera at Mayerling
1890   Resignation of German chancellor Bismarck; cancellation of reinsurance treaty between Germany and Russia
1891   Franco-Russian proposals for consultation in event of European war, leading to secret alliance to counter Austro-German-Italian alliance
1894   Death of Alexander III of Russia and accession of Nicholas II
1896   Third meeting of Queen Victoria and Francis Joseph; death of Charles Ludwig, brother of emperor

1897	Last meeting between Queen Victoria and Francis Joseph; Greek-Turkish war; Queen Victoria's diamond jubilee, at which Habsburgs are represented by Francis Ferdinand
1898	Assassination of Elizabeth at Geneva overshadows Francis Joseph's golden jubilee festivities
1899	Outbreak of Boer war
1900	Morganatic marriage of Francis Ferdinand and Countess Sophie Chotek, created princess of Hohenberg
1901	Death of Queen Victoria and accession of King Edward VII
1903	State visit of Edward VII to Vienna
1904	Visit of prince and princess of Wales to Vienna; first of regular visits of Edward VII to Marienbad and Ischl for informal meetings with Francis Joseph
1908	Austrian annexation of Bosnia and Herzegovina
1910	Death of Edward VII and accession of George V; funeral attended by Francis Ferdinand
1911	Coronation of George V attended by Charles; marriage of Charles and Zita of Bourbon-Parma
1912	First Balkan war; first joint visit of Francis Ferdinand and Sophie to England
1913	Second Balkian war; second visit of Francis Ferdinand and Sophie to England
1914	Assassination of Francis Ferdinand and Sophie at Sarajevo; Serbia's rejection of Austrian ultimatum leads to outbreak of Great War, with Great Britain's declaration of war on Germany and later Austria
1916	Death of Francis Joseph and accession of Charles
1917	Overthrow of Romanov dynasty and Russian revolution; peace initiative launched by Charles and Sixtus of Bourbon-Parma
1918	Renunciation by Charles of dual alliance and signing of armistice with Britain and France, followed by his abdication and that of William II in Germany
1919	Charles and family move to Switzerland
1921	Charles returns to Hungary, but after failure of coup moves to Madeira
1922	Death of Charles

Reference Notes

RA – Royal Archives, Windsor

CHAPTER 1 (pp. 13–29)

1 Ashley Vol. 1 104
2 Ridley 344
3 Connell 74
4 Ashley Vol. 1 98
5 Ridley 348
6 Redlich 49
7 Marek 109
8 Bennett, *King without a crown* 205
9 RA F24/105
10 RA F24/140
11 RA F25/72
12 RA I27/13
13 *Letters of the Prince Consort* 187
14 Marek 81
15 as 14
16 *Letters of Queen Victoria* Series I Vol. ii 447–48 (hereafter *Letters QV*)
17 Ibid 448

CHAPTER 2 (pp. 30–48)

1 *Letters QV* I iii 211
2 Haslip, *Imperial adventurer* 83
3 Ibid 84–85
4 Martin Vol. 4 59
5 as 4
6 Ibid 58
7 RA I30/82
8 RA I30/83
9 Martin Vol. 4 342
10 RA I30/81
11 Aronson, *Queen Victoria and the Bonapartes* 95
12 Crankshaw 98
13 Bennett, *King without a crown* 339–40
14 *The Times* 22.11.1916
15 Haslip, *Imperial adventurer* 121
16 Martin Vol. 5 161
17 *Letters QV* I iii 408
18 Ibid 409
19 RA I33/43
20 *Letters QV* I iii 407–8
21 *Dearest Child* 282
22 Ibid 285
23 Martin Vol. 5 415
24 Ibid 373
25 Ibid 385

CHAPTER 3 (pp. 49–63)

1 RA M65/1
2 Lee, *King Edward VII* Vol. 1 132
3 Corti, *English Empress* 98
4 Ibid 99
5 Crankshaw 81
6 Haslip, *Lonely Empress* 170
7 *Dearest Mama* 262–63
8 Ibid 264
9 *Letters QV* II i 110
10 *Dearest Mama* 319
11 Corti, *English Empress* 141
12 *Your dear letter* 61
13 *Letters QV* II i 311
14 *Your dear letter* 95–96
15 Brook-Shepherd, *Uncle of Europe* 80
16 Marek 187
17 *Your dear letter* 103
18 *Letters QV* II i 441

CHAPTER 4 (pp. 64–88)

1 *Darling Child* 91
2 RA Z451/162
3,4 as 2
5 Lee, *King Edward VII* Vol. 1 356
6 *Darling Child* 145
7 as 6
8 Rose 2–3
9 Corti, *Elizabeth* 208
10 RA L26/115
11 RA L26/116
12 Corti, *Elizabeth* 210
13 RA I50/27
14 *Darling Child* 205–6

15 Corti, *Elizabeth* 222
16 RA Add A2/33
17 Barkeley 44
18 RA I51/111
19 RA I87/74
20 *Darling Child* 68

CHAPTER 5 (pp. 89–107)

1   Barkeley 61
2   Listowel 106
3   Ibid 121
4   Stephanie of Belgium 21–22
5   *Letters of the Empress Frederick* 210–11
6   Stephanie of Belgium 210
7   Mitis 372
8   Barkeley 184
9   *Letters QV* III i 400
10 William II 229–30
11 Listowel 183
12 Cassels 185
13 Brook-Shepherd, *Uncle of Europe* 77
14 Magnus, *King Edward the Seventh* 210
15 RA GV AA17/42
16 as 15
17 *Letters QV* III i 440–41
18 St Aubyn 283
19 Haslip, *Lonely Empress* 404
20 RA Z498/56
21 Barkeley 285

CHAPTER 6 (pp. 108–115)

1   RA GV AA18/33
2   *The Times* 10.7.1891
3   Corti, *Elizabeth* 355
4   Marek 365
5   *Letters QV* III iii 145
6   Eisenmenger 172
7   Margutti 117
8   Ibid 119
9   *Letters QV* III iii 174
10 *Empress Frederick writes to Sophie* 253
11 Eisenmenger 190
12 RA I88/45
13 RA I88/49
14 RA I88/69

15 *Martyrdom of an Empress* 266
16 Corti, *English Empress* 357
17 Margutti 70

CHAPTER 7 (pp. 116–136)

1   *Letters QV* III iii 637
2   Haslip, *Emperor and the actress* 256
3   RA GV AA23/46
4   Pope-Hennessy 385
5   Ibid 386
6   Gore 189
7   Pope-Hennessy 386–87
8   Margutti 210
9   Brook-Shepherd, *Uncle of Europe* 292
10 Ibid 296
11 Magnus, *King Edward the Seventh* 395
12 Brook-Shepherd, *Uncle of Europe* 306
13 Margutti 225
14 Redlich 510
15 Brook-Shepherd, *Uncle of Europe* 311
16 Ibid 312
17 RA W54/70
18 Lee, *King Eaward VII* Vol. 2 634
19 RA W54/103
20 Redlich 519
21 Lee, *King Edward VII* Vol. 2 664
22 Margutti 267
23 Ibid 267–68

CHAPTER 8 (pp. 137–156)

1   Brook-Shepherd, *Victims at Sarajevo* 209
2   Gore 287
3   Fisher 1115–16
4   Rose 170
5   Ibid 171
6   Margutti 266
7   *The Times* 24.7.1984
8   RA, Journal of King George V 23.11.1916
9   *The Times* 22.11.1916
10 11 as 9
12 Brook-Shepherd, *Last Habsburg* 87
13 Ibid 89
14 *The Times* 3.4.1922

Bibliography

MANUSCRIPT SOURCES

Royal Archives, Windsor. Correspondence between Queen Victoria and Emperor Francis Joseph, 1851–98; between Queen Victoria and Empress Elizabeth, 1874–79; between King Edward VII (as Prince of Wales, and as King) and Emperor Francis Joseph, 1862–1908; between Queen Victoria and the Prince of Wales, 1873–89; between Edward VII (as Prince and King) and Prince George (later King George V), 1888–1903; Journal of King George V

PRINTED SOURCES

(1) British and German royalty

ALBERT, Prince Consort *Letters of the Prince Consort, 1831–1861*; selected and edited by Kurt Jagow (John Murray 1938)

AMES, Winslow *Prince Albert and Victorian taste* (Chapman & Hall 1967)

ARONSON, Theo *Queen Victoria and the Bonapartes* (Cassell 1972)

ASHDOWN, Dulcie M. *Victoria and the Coburgs* (Robert Hale 1981)

BATTISCOMBE, Georgina *Queen Alexandra* (Constable 1969)

BENNETT, Daphne *King without a crown: Albert, Prince Consort of England, 1819–1861* (Heinemann 1977)

—— *Vicky, Princess Royal of England and German Empress* (Collins Harvill 1971)

BROOK-SHEPHERD, Gordon *Uncle of Europe: the social and diplomatic life of Edward VII* (Collins 1975)

CORTI, Egon Caesar Conte *The English Empress: a study in the relations between Queen Victoria and her eldest daughter, Empress Frederick of Germany* (Cassell 1957)

EYCK, Frank *The Prince Consort: a political biography* (Chatto & Windus 1959)

GORE, John *King George V, a personal memoir* (John Murray 1941)

LEE, Sir Sidney *King Edward VII*, 2 vols. (Macmillan 1925–27)

—— *Queen Victoria: a biography* (Smith, Elder 1902)

LONGFORD, Elizabeth *Victoria R.I.* (Weidenfeld & Nicolson 1964)

MAGNUS, Philip *King Edward the Seventh* (John Murray 1964)

MARTIN, Theodore *The life of His Royal Highness the Prince Consort*, 5 vols. (Smith, Elder 1874–80)

POPE-HENNESSY, James *Queen Mary 1867–1953* (Allen & Unwin 1959)

ROSE, Kenneth *King George V* (Weidenfeld & Nicolson 1983)

ST AUBYN, Giles *Edward VII, Prince and King* (Collins 1979)

VAN DER KISTE, John *Frederick III, German Emperor 1888* (Alan Sutton 1981)

VICTORIA, Consort of Frederick III, German Emperor *The Empress Frederick writes to Sophie, her daughter, Crown Princess and later Queen of the Hellenes: letters, 1889–1901*; edited by Arthur Gould Lee (Faber 1955)

—— *Letters of the Empress Frederick*; edited by Sir Frederick Ponsonby (Macmillan 1928)

VICTORIA, Queen *The letters of Queen Victoria: a selection from Her Majesty's correspondence between the years 1837 and 1861*; edited by A.C. Benson and Viscount Esher, 3 vols. (John Murray 1907)

—— *The letters of Queen Victoria, second series: a selection from Her Majesty's correspondence and journal between the years 1862 and 1885*; edited by George Earle Buckle, 3 vols. (John Murray 1926–28)

—— *The letters of Queen Victoria, third series: a selection from Her Majesty's correspondence the journal between the years 1886 and 1901*; edited by G.E. Buckle, 3 vols. (John Murray 1930–32)

VICTORIA, Queen, and VICTORIA, Consort of Frederick III *Dearest Child: letters between Queen Victoria and the Princess Royal, 1858–1861*; edited by Roger Fulford (Evans Bros 1964)

—— *Dearest Mama: letters between Queen Victoria and the Crown Princess of Prussia, 1862–1864*; edited by Roger Fulford (Evans Bros 1968)

—— *Your dear letter: private correspondence between Queen Victoria and the Crown Princess of Prussia, 1865–1871*; edited by Roger Fulford (Evans Bros 1971)

—— *Darling Child: private correspondence of Queen Victoria and the Crown Princess of Prussia, 1871–1878*; edited by Roger Fulford (Evans Bros 1976)

—— *Beloved Mama: private correspondence of Queen Victoria and the Crown Princess of Prussia, 1878–1885*; edited by Roger Fulford (Evans Bros 1981)

WILLIAM II, Ex-German Emperor *My early life* (Methuen 1926)

(2)   Austrian royalty

Anon. *The martyrdom of an Empress* [Elizabeth] (Harper 1899) Author believed to be Margaret Cunliffe-Owen

BARKELEY, Richard *The road to Mayerling: life and death of Crown Prince Rudolph of Austria* (Macmillan 1958)

BASSETT, Richard *Mayerling prince 'murdered by French agents'* (in *The Times* 20 December 1983)

BROOK-SHEPHERD, Gordon *The last Habsburg* [Charles] (Weidenfeld & Nicolson 1968)

—— *Victims at Sarajevo: the romance and tragedy of Franz Ferdinand and Sophie* (Harvill 1984)

CASSELS, Lavender *Clash of generations: a Habsburg family drama in the nineteenth century* (John Murray 1973)

CORTI, Egon Caesar Conte *Elizabeth, Empress of Austria* (Thornton Butterworth 1936)

CRANKSHAW, Edward *The fall of the house of Habsburg* (Longman 1963)

EISENMENGER, Victor *Archduke Francis Ferdinand* (Selwyn & Blount 1931)

HASLIP, Joan *The Emperor and the actress: the love story of Emperor Franz Josef and Katharina Schratt* (Weidenfeld & Nicolson 1982)

—— *Imperial adventurer: Emperor Maximilian of Mexico and his Empress* (Weidenfeld & Nicolson 1971)

—— *The lonely Empress: a biography of Elizabeth of Austria* (Weidenfeld & Nicolson 1965)

HOLMES, T.J.D. *Franz Joseph recalled* (letter in *The Times* 24 July 1984)

HYDE, H. Montgomery *Mexican Empire: the history of Maximilian and Carlota of Mexico* (Macmillan 1946)

JUDTMANN, Fritz *Mayerling: the facts behind the legend* (Harrap 1971)

KETTERL, Eugen *The Emperor Francis Joseph I: an intimate study* (Skeffington 1929)

LISTOWEL, Judith *A Habsburg tragedy: Crown Prince Rudolf* (Ascent 1978)

MAREK, George R. *The eagles die: Franz Joseph, Elizabeth, and their Austria* (Hart-Davis, MacGibbon 1975)

MARGUTTI, Lieutenant-General Baron von *The Emperor Francis Joseph and his times* (Hutchinson 1921)

MITIS, Oscar von, Baron *The life of the Crown Prince Rudolph of Habsburg* (Skeffington 1930)

PAULI, Hertha *The secret of Sarajevo: the story of Franz Ferdinand and Sophie* (Collins 1966)

REDLICH, Joseph *Emperor Francis Joseph of Austria: a biography* (Macmillan 1929)

STEPHANIE of Belgium, Princess *I was to be Empress* (Ivor Nicholson & Watson 1937)

TSCHUPPIK, Karl *The Empress Elizabeth of Austria* (Constable 1930)

VAN DER KISTE, John *An Empress at Steephill Castle* (in *Hampshire County Magazine* August 1979)

WELCOME, John *The Sporting Empress: the story of Elizabeth of Austria and Bay Middleton* (Michael Joseph 1975)

It is significant that Emperor Francis Joseph has attracted less biographers, in English at least, than his wife, son, brother and nephew, whose eccentricities and violent deaths have rendered them more interesting for the general reader. If one excludes Haslip's *The Emperor and the actress*, and Marek's *The eagles die* (which the author requests in his Foreword to be treated as biography, not history), there are only three studies of the Emperor, all published soon after his death. Each is useful in its own way, but Redlich's is probably the most historically accurate. Those by Margutti and Ketterl, both of whom knew their subject well, suffer not unnaturally from lack of objectivity. An English translation of Ottokar Janetschek's *The Emperor Franz Joseph* (Laurie 1953) purports to be biography but reads like a work of fiction and is not recommended. Egon Caesar Conte Corti's three-volume *Franz Joseph* and a one-volume work written with

Hans Sokol, all published in Graz between 1950 and 1960, have never been published in English.

(3)   General

ARONSON, Theo *Crowns in Conflict: triumph and tragedy of European monarchy, 1910–18* (John Murray 1986)

ASHLEY, Evelyn *The life of H.J. Temple, Viscount Palmerston, 1846–65: with selections from his speeches and correspondence,* 2 vols. (Bentley 1876)

BLAKE, Robert *Disraeli* (Eyre & Spottiswoode 1966)

CECIL, Algernon *Queen Victoria and her Prime Ministers* (Eyre & Spottiswoode 1953)

CONNELL, Brian *Regina v. Palmerston: the correspondence between Queen Victoria and her Foreign and Prime Minister 1837–1865* (Evans Bros 1962)

DUFF, David *Eugenie and Napoleon III* (Collins 1978)

FISHER, H.A.L. *A history of Europe* (Edward Arnold 1936)

MACARTNEY, C.A. *The Habsburg empire 1790–1918* (Weidenfeld & Nicolson 1968)

MAGNUS, Philip *Gladstone: a biography* (John Murray 1954)

PURNELL's HISTORY of the 20th Century, 9 vols. (New Caxton Library Service 1971–72)

RIDLEY, Jasper *Lord Palmerston* (Constable 1970)

SZEPS, Berta [Frau Szeps-Zuckerkandl] *My life and history* (Cassell 1938)

The Times – various references 1848–1984

Index

Kings, queens, princes and princesses are of Great Britain; emperors, empresses, archdukes and archduchesses are of Austria (or Austria-Hungary) unless stated otherwise